May God bless you
for blessing me!
        Eden Kelley
        Psalm 34:18

PRISON DIVA

Eden Kelley

Copyright © 2016 Eden Kelley.

All rights reserved. No part of this book may be used or reproduced by any means, graphic, electronic, or mechanical, including photocopying, recording, taping or by any information storage retrieval system without the written permission of the author except in the case of brief quotations embodied in critical articles and reviews.

Scriptures taken from the Holy Bible, New International Version®, NIV®. Copyright © 1973, 1978, 1984, 2011 by Biblica, Inc.™ Used by permission of Zondervan. All rights reserved worldwide. www.zondervan.com The "NIV" and "New International Version" are trademarks registered in the United States Patent and Trademark Office by Biblica, Inc.™

Archway Publishing books may be ordered through booksellers or by contacting:

Archway Publishing
1663 Liberty Drive
Bloomington, IN 47403
www.archwaypublishing.com
1 (888) 242-5904

Because of the dynamic nature of the Internet, any web addresses or links contained in this book may have changed since publication and may no longer be valid. The views expressed in this work are solely those of the author and do not necessarily reflect the views of the publisher, and the publisher hereby disclaims any responsibility for them.

Any people depicted in stock imagery provided by Thinkstock are models, and such images are being used for illustrative purposes only. Certain stock imagery © Thinkstock.

ISBN: 978-1-4808-4028-7 (sc)
ISBN: 978-1-4808-4030-0 (hc)
ISBN: 978-1-4808-4029-4 (e)

Library of Congress Control Number: 2016919551

Print information available on the last page.

Archway Publishing rev. date: 12/6/2016

Contents

Prologue vii

Chapter 1	Introduction 1
Chapter 2	"Let Me Introduce ..." 5
Chapter 3	"What's Wrong with Me?" 9
Chapter 4	A Wall and Plastic Flowers 22
Chapter 5	Actions Speak Louder Than Words ... Or Do They? 46
Chapter 6	Got Ministry? 64
Chapter 7	The Final Impact 88
Chapter 8	The Unraveling 102
Chapter 9	The End of the Beginning 107
Chapter 10	The Long Journey Back 112
Chapter 11	Mirror Image 117
Chapter 12	The New Beginning 125

Epilogue 129

Prologue

The room was poorly lit, and the round table was full of half-empty glasses. She was surrounded by unfamiliar faces and listening to voices she didn't recognize, a scene not too uncommon for her. As she sat there, she chuckled under her breath. She had no idea what this gathering was about. It all seemed rather odd. She glanced up from taking a sip of her drink and noticed a display of lights on a large stage farther down from where she was sitting. The large red velvet drapes that majestically framed the old wooden theater seemed to be in rivalry with the contemporary light show that was being rehearsed. She soon lost all interest in the conversations at the table and focused on the stage. Unexpectedly, she heard someone call her name from the end of the table and then say, "Eden, you have to hurry so you won't be late for your hair appointment!"

"Me? Why do I have a hair appointment?" she replied as she ran her fingers through her hair, not wanting to get anything done to it. She liked her hair just the way it was!

The person insisted. "You have to go now! You are the Prison Diva!" Confusion set in as she tried to determine what was happening, but bewilderment quickly turned to excitement with the realization that she was going to be a diva ... the Prison Diva!

She arrived at the salon to meet with her new hairdresser. He was very informal and seemed to know exactly what he needed to do for the Prison Diva. She was so excited yet nervous. She was ready for a change. The man began to cut her hair as she looked at various wild hair colors and styles. She was the Prison Diva! Everything must be perfect! Before she knew it, he was finished. He spun her around in the salon chair so she could see the changes he had made. "Is that it? No brilliant red or blazing black? No crazy stripes? Just a cut?" Eden asked.

"Yes, that is it," he answered without expression. She didn't understand. She thought the Prison Diva was surely an important role.

Sorely disappointed, Eden asked her hairdresser, "Just who *is* the Prison Diva anyway?"

His reply was disconcerting. "She is the one who—"

She woke up.

Chapter 1

Introduction

THE CEILING FAN HAD not moved in days. The dust on each blade was starting to unnerve her. On the wall hung a portrait of her grandmother as a young woman sitting on a piano bench, wearing a gorgeous red dress that draped to the floor. The old grand piano was beautifully displayed in front of a fireplace framed with antique photographs. The picture brought back many memories of her godly grandmother, whom she still missed. Eden gazed back at the woman in the picture and began to cry aloud, "Lord, I am so lonely! My phone doesn't ring, and no one comes by. I just have to lie here!" Three days post-back surgery, and depression had hit. To be completely honest, she was sulking and drowning in self-pity. Eden's past started to haunt her as anger, resentment, guilt, and painful memories overwhelmed her. She began to pour her heart out to God. "I did all the right things, Lord," she cried. "So why did it happen to me? What did I do wrong? I tried to live for you!"

Eden had been raised in a wonderful Christian home. The Lord could not have blessed her more. She heard the truth of the gospel every day as her parents lived it, spoke it, walked it, and taught it. She accepted Christ as her Lord and Savior at the age of six. As a teenager, she tried very hard to do all the right things. She was always in church—Sunday morning and Sunday night, visitation on Tuesday night, choir and Bible study on Wednesday night, vacation Bible school every summer, and weekly youth group meetings. She was musically talented and often asked to be the featured soloist for various events, both small and large.

As time progressed, she was given leadership roles in women's ministries and youth events. She also began traveling to other states, sharing the gospel through song and music. *The Lord is blessing me for being faithful*, she thought. Eden was diligent in trying to live her life according to the Bible, attempting to follow the principles she had been taught from childhood. Now inner turmoil, anger, self-destruction, hurt, confusion, and revenge were raging inside of her. Her life did not turn out the way she had planned or dreamed it would. Eden was aware that other people had lived through greater and more troublesome situations than she had, but she was still heavily burdened and hurt by the circumstances she had faced in her life.

God has me on my back for a reason, she thought. She was exhausted from yelling at God, "Why me?" She was unable to shake the feelings of extreme loneliness. Her mind started racing with memories of what she used to do and who she used to be. "I lost everything, Lord," she cried. "I don't know how to get it back—my home, family, integrity, trust, faith, song, and ministry." Feeling so ashamed, she decided to ask the Lord if He would restore her, so she began to pray. But it was different this time. As Eden lay on her back in her bed, she had no other option but to look up. With her eyes open and her heart torn, Eden's communication with the Lord began. It seemed as though she talked out loud for hours. It was amazing how much she could say when no one was there to interrupt her. But then there was silence; no more words, just tears. She lay there, looking up at the ceiling, pondering the string of events that had brought her to this place. For years, Eden had held in the anger and bitterness about where her life's journey had taken her. It was time to restore her heart, soul, mind, and body if God was ever going to use her again. Under Eden's bed lay a heart-shaped box that contained her diaries that she had kept since she was a little girl. It was as if God whispered to her, "Read them," so Eden took the old box from beneath the bed and began reading all nine diaries from the very beginning. Sleep normally eluded her, but tonight she slept.

She awoke the next morning feeling that her "talk" with God had been quite therapeutic. She spent some time reading a good book, written by a pastor who meant a lot to her. She searched for programs on television to encourage and strengthen her. Things were somewhat different today, but when she tried to pray, she didn't have as much to say. Was she good to go? Had God healed the brokenness and restored her relationship with Him? Then the feelings of frustration and anger resurfaced, and she soon found herself staring at the ceiling as the tears started to flow. She wanted them to stop! In desperation, she cried out again, "Lord, I want my life back! Why am I afraid to ask for my old life back ... the life where You used me to teach, sing, and speak? Why do I still feel ashamed after You have delivered, cleansed, and forgiven me? I can't get past the past!"

She lay there with anticipation, expecting some miraculous answer to be delivered through a lightning bolt, but instead she heard a gentle voice saying, "Be still, and know that I am God!"

Eden had to laugh. Of course! She was not *listening* to the Lord; she was *talking* to Him—a one-way conversation, and it was all about her. She had been praying for years that the Lord would deliver her from the bondage in which she had put herself, that He would in some way use her again. She thought she was making great strides toward putting the past behind her. Now God was asking her to be still. This was her biggest obstacle. She *would not* and *could not* be still.

"Be still, and know that I am God" (Psalm 46:10). Why are

such simple words so difficult to carry out? She had to come to a complete stop so her body could heal after surgery. The Lord had to stop her in her tracks and put her on her back to get her attention. She had been going about her daily routine, believing in her finite mind that she was doing an outstanding job in moving forward in her walk with Christ. She was praying every day, reading her Bible, and trying to minister to those around her. However, when the slightest adversity came, she found that she was empty, still bitter, and very angry. She was going nowhere fast and didn't understand why. Perhaps it would be helpful to revisit her childhood and the string of events that brought her to this point in her life. Could it be that she needed to identify any factors that might have contributed to all those years of self-destruction?

Chapter 2

"Let Me Introduce …"

Eden was in the middle of her sixth-grade year when she moved to another new city. Her heart was breaking when she stood in front of the large double window of their new two-story home. It overlooked many well-groomed houses that were neatly lined with sidewalks on either side of the street. She had moved from the Midwest where her neighborhood did not have any sidewalks, just gravel roads and horse trails. She had lived in neighborhoods that had sidewalks before, but she really loved living in the mountains where she could play in the woods and run free, away from the noise of city life. It was a gloomy day, and she noticed that no one was walking on the sidewalks, and no children were playing outdoors. Their moving boxes were out near the driveway for the garbage truck to pick up the next day. She was always the first to have everything unpacked and put away neatly in its place. Moving was not new to her. She had lost count of how many times she had packed and unpacked. Eden's family was in the ministry, and they normally moved every two to four years, but this time seemed to be the most difficult for her. Eden stared out the window and began to cry, her heart hurting beyond description. She had left her best friends *once more*. The thought of never seeing them again felt like a death. Tomorrow would be Eden's first day in another new school.

"Class, let me introduce to you our new student, Eden. She just moved here, so please make her feel welcome." She had heard those words so many times! She had stood in front of too many classrooms, being introduced as the "new student" and watching the faces of the kids in front of her. They seemed to be absolutely emotionless. "They don't care who I am or where I came from," she told herself. She would wait for others to introduce themselves to her, but it seldom happened.

She was very quiet and shy in demeanor. She was the new kid. *I shouldn't have to introduce myself to them*, she thought. She could see the kids whisper and giggle as they stared at her. It was usually her accent, her clothes, or her hair. Styles and accents were different, varying from state to state. It didn't help matters when they found out that she was the "preacher's kid." She was a year older than the other students. She had to repeat the third grade after the last move, because she was so far behind in the curriculum. Every state was different in teaching techniques and courses of study—an additional challenge she had to face with each move.

She always dreaded the long walk to the cafeteria. What was it about the smell? It was universal. She had been in many cafeterias across the nation, and they all smelled the same! How could that be? It was comical but very stressful. Oh, how she dreaded lunchtime! Where was she going to sit? Was anyone going to ask her to sit with them? Then, of course, what follows lunchtime? Yes … recess, and she had the same dilemma. She would wander around alone on the playground, not having friends to play with. In an effort to blend into the background, she would often pull the hood of her coat up over her head, putting her hands deep into her pockets. As she watched the other kids play, she just walked and thought about her old friends. Eden was always relieved at the sound of the bell; it somehow lifted the pressure of being alone during recess.

Eden began walking toward her classroom after recess when she suddenly stopped in her tracks. There she was, Mia, sitting on the front steps, blocking the front door of the classroom. She was a tall girl with blonde hair and a large frame. Mia did not like Eden for some reason and chose to make fun of Eden's hair and face, her clothes and accent. Mia even started a club with all the other girls in the class and told Eden if she wanted to be a part of the club, she would have to pay a fee. Of course, Eden did not have any money, and she knew Mia had formed the club specifically to keep her out. Eden had difficulty in the past making friends, but never had she encountered someone quite as cruel.

She would hold in her tears, but in doing so, anger began to fester. She just wanted the other kids to like her and accept her! What was she doing wrong and why didn't they like her? Eden's mother would stand her in front of the bathroom mirror and ask Eden, "Honey, what do you see?" Eden's reply, "Nothing." Her mother would ask again, "No, honey, I see a beautiful young girl with a healthy body, pretty eyes, long, pretty hair, a gorgeous smile, and pretty skin! What do you see?" Eden's reply was, "Nothing." Her mother would try so hard to help Eden see how beautiful she was and how blessed she was. Eden saw nothing in herself and didn't feel as though other people saw anything in her either. With no other outlet for expressing her feelings, she began to write in a diary. Every day, she would sit alone in her room and tell the diary just how she felt. It became a silent friend, and it was a way for her to share stories and feelings she would not tell anyone else. So day after day, she wrote in her diary and frequently cried herself to sleep.

January 1980
Dear Diary,

Today was my first day at my new school. I hate it. I'm so homesick I could actually throw up! I cry and cry. I do hope and pray that I get used to it!

Eden had lived in seven states, from the West Coast to the East Coast, and had attended sixteen different schools. In fact, she had traveled to over twenty-two states by the time she was six months old. In spite of the travel and constant relocations, she greatly admired her father and mother. Their dedicated, selfless service to God and others left an indelible impression on her life.

She recalled many times when her dad would drive the car onto the gravel parking lot of a church—often a small, redbrick church with a white steeple. They would sit in the car for about twenty minutes so her dad could review his message before the morning service. As they waited, there was too much time for Eden's mind to think and her stomach to turn into knots. Her heart would start to race, and she just wanted to cry. She didn't want to go in! She didn't know anyone ... again! She didn't want to be introduced to everyone ... again. She didn't want to gaze into strangers' faces or watch them whisper. She was tired of wondering what they were thinking.

"We need to go on in," Eden's dad would say, and she would immediately feel sick. She would paste on a smile and act as though she felt fine. She held her head up high and occupied a seat in the front row with her mother. There was always an opening announcement, about three congregational hymns, and the choir would sing. Sometimes her mom would sing and play the piano. She had such a beautiful voice, and Eden loved to hear her. Following the music, her dad, whom she admired and loved to hear, would preach.

Chapter 3

———————————— ————————————

"What's Wrong with Me?"

1980
Dear Diary,

Today I surrendered my life to Jesus. And hope to become a missionary. But I think he wants me to become a missionary. And I'm proud that I surrendered my life to him!

EDEN WAS A TEENAGER now. She knew she was a Christian and wanted to uphold her personal values and convictions, but she now struggled with her need to be accepted by others. Her physical appearance was not what she desired. She began struggling with her weight and severe cystic acne. She had mood swings that could not be explained. Some mornings, she would awaken with her eyes almost shut because her face was unusually swollen. The cystic acne would be so severe it would leak uncontrollably. She began wearing heavy makeup to cover, or mask, the oozing sores. Her body was suddenly turning into a medical mystery. She seemed to have no control over her moods, weight, or skin problems. Her parents sought medical help from many doctors, trying to find a solution. She started exercising and watching what she ate. No one ever referred to her as being "fat." Instead, they used words like "puffy." Her face was very swollen and round, some days more than others. Eden's attitude became worse, and her parents thought that drugs could be causing her severe mood swings. Eden's life was spiraling out of control, and no one could explain why.

Eden had moved a couple of times during her high school years, from the West Coast to the far tips of the southern shore. This was an exciting move for her! Who, as a teenager, would not want to move to the beach? She was in the middle of her sophomore year, but this time she was excited for the change. It was another culture shock moving from one side of the United States to the other but a change Eden adjusted to quite nicely. Her high school was much larger, and she had to walk outside to her classrooms. That was a new concept, and with the hot, humid weather, it was difficult to get used to. However, Eden felt as though she blended in here more than any other place she had ever lived. It was a melting pot of all cultures, accents, and styles, with new people moving to and from the beach every day. Not to mention all of the tourists consistently passing through; new faces were common. For the very first time, Eden felt as though she had found her home.

Churches were few and far between in the cities where she had previously lived. Now the churches were everywhere! It was refreshing for her to be surrounded by a church on every corner, and the choices seemed endless! Her family had been invited to visit a very large church that was located downtown. They had always been members of very small churches where she and her brother were sometimes the only youth. This church had several hundred young people in the youth group! She and her parents were eager to join the church. Eden immediately became involved in the youth choir, youth Sunday school, Tuesday night visitation, and any other activity the church had to offer. She was soon a frequent soloist in the youth choir, Sunday school services, and both morning and evening church services. God was choosing to bless her far more than she could have ever imagined. She was gaining encouragement as a Christian and as a young woman, like never before.

God began to open doors of opportunities for Eden to sing in other churches, at local youth conventions, and at other area events. However, Eden had a recurring hindrance, or obstacle, when she sang. She would either forget or make up her words every time! She had an exciting opportunity to sing at a local youth convention. She was looking forward to it; however, memorizing the words of the songs for Eden was very stressful. She knew how forgetful she became when nerves overwhelmed her during her performance. She appreciated every opportunity given to her, and she always prepared to give her best.

The arena was full of young people from all over the state. Eden stood anxiously behind the theater drapes as she stared at the hardwood floor of the large stage. The walk across the old platform to the microphone seemed miles away. The lights were so bright that the faces in the crowd became ghostly. She could hear the yells and laughter of all the teenagers in the audience. She loved the powerful energy of youth conferences; they were exhilarating, and the after effects were contagious! She loved the enthusiasm it generated within her and others. However, this time she was not a participant but a performer. Then she heard, "I would like to introduce ..." and Eden nervously walked onto the stage while the music began to play. Eden took hold of the microphone, and as she started to sing, she began making up every word! How was this happening? What was she even saying? She was humiliated and appalled, knowing she had spent weeks preparing for this major event. Eden humbly finished her song and quickly exited the stage. She was astonished by the audience feedback but still hoping no one had noticed that she made up the words to her song. After the conference, not one person mentioned anything about her errors made in the song. It was as if God had deafened their ears to her mistakes and orchestrated His own lyrics for the audience to hear. Eden was blessed and humbled by what God had done for her.

However, Eden was starting to get an inferiority complex. It did not matter how many times she rehearsed a song; nerves and feelings of inadequacy would overwhelm her. The need to perfect each song and performance became somewhat discouraging and stressful. The emphasis on the memorization and the demands for perfection of each song caused her to become misconstrued in her heart and in her head. For whom she was really singing—God or people? Soon all that mattered to her was the response of those that had asked her to sing and, of course, the audience. Once again, she began allowing her self-worth to form around the opinions and reactions of people she knew and even by others she would never see again. Her self-worth was based solely on her talent, abilities, or lack thereof.

Outside of church life, her high school years were fine. She took her Bible to school, and her closest friendships were those from her church youth group. She did her best to walk the narrow road and live a life pleasing to God and her biblical convictions. She was truly happy in Jesus and with her many Christian friends. However, she had inner struggles with the mystery medical condition that seemed to be worsening and haunting her every day. It started to interfere with her social life. The acne, open sores on her face, facial swelling, and weight issue made it very difficult for her. She begged not to go to church or school sometimes, just out of embarrassment. It was very frustrating; however, she had to keep active with her singing opportunities, youth events, and school. Eden didn't have a jacket with a hood to cover her face anymore, like she did as a little girl. She now found herself hiding behind a lot of makeup, big hair, and the clothes she wore. She began to be overly conscious about what she was eating, hoping to lose weight and perhaps look more appealing to her peers. Frustrated and desperate, she was still trusting that God would deliver her from this disease or whatever it was.

January 19, 1984
Dear Diary,

You know, I look back and wonder why I did and didn't do some things! I'm ashamed of a lot of it, but it is part of growing up and learning! I wouldn't want anyone to read this. It's so depressing and shameful! I can't change the past, but I'll change my future for the best! Some people think it is great to keep a diary, and I guess it is, but if I were to die before I threw this junk book away, what would happen to it? Who would read it? I want to throw it away, but I like to look back and learn from things I've done in the past! Ya know! I hope whoever reads this won't be ashamed of me or surprised!

9-11-85
Dear Diary,

Today I stayed home from school. See, yesterday my lip swelled, for no reason! I went to school. But today it's worse. I'm going to the doctor. I hope it goes away before church! Bye.

Eden was a senior year in high school when a family friend asked her if she would be interested in participating in a preliminary for the local county pageant. She had never been interested in doing a pageant before. From her point of view, there was nothing attractive about her, so the thought never entered her mind. Someone must be seeing something she didn't see! Reluctantly, she agreed to participate, because this particular pageant offered a college scholarship to the winner. If she could win a scholarship, it would definitely be worth it! The pageant was scheduled late in the year, and Eden only had a few weeks to prepare. She found a Christian song she wanted to sing for her talent and bought a formal dress for the evening gown competition and a swimsuit for the swimwear competition. Eden began exercising more, dieting, and reading newspapers to catch up on current events. This was an awesome opportunity! When the big night arrived, she was finally ready.

Once again, Eden was standing to the side entrance of the stage, but this time, the questions in her mind were overwhelming. *What am I doing here? Who would vote for me?* Suddenly, it became just another stage, under different circumstances, and she was there for different reasons. Regardless, the same nervous, gut-wrenching emotions overwhelmed her as she walked onto the stage to sing. She composed herself, painted on a smile, took hold of the microphone, and sang her song beautifully as she had done many times before, but this time Eden made it through her song without any mistakes! What a miracle!

As the time approached for the winner to be announced, she remembered thinking, *How nice it would be to have a crown!* Eden had never won anything. The judges called all the girls to the front of the stage. With nervous smiles, they stood in a single line across the stage. The lights were so bright you could not see one face in the audience, nor could you hear a pin drop. Then she heard the judges announce the winner. "We would like to introduce to you the next Miss ... Eden ..." She won first place! This was surreal! She had actually won! As tears ran down her puffy cheeks, she stood in complete amazement and cried. She could not believe that what had begun as a frivolous adventure, God had used to surpass any expectations she could have ever imagined.

Eden went home that evening completely amazed. All the mental and physical disillusionment that had burdened her was suddenly lifted. The judges saw something in her that she failed to see in herself! She cried herself to sleep that night, not because of loneliness or disappointment. This time she felt secure and confident from within—a very uncommon feeling for her. She was going to represent her county, and she wanted to do it God's way. She only had a few months to prepare for the Miss America preliminary. Three ladies from the county pageant were assigned to help her prepare for the state pageant. She had to purchase a new wardrobe and follow a strict diet and exercise program to lose weight. She met with these ladies every day after school to exercise, shop for pageant clothes, practice walking and turning on the stage, and rehearse interview questions. Eden worked very hard to do all they instructed her to do. The weight, however, was not budging. In fact, some days she looked "puffier," as she was told. It was frustrating to everyone involved. She knew it was from her medical condition but did not know what was causing it. Her doctor prescribed medications, but nothing worked.

January 28, 1986
Dear Diary,

I don't understand why no one has ever asked me out from my HS? Not that there is anyone I want to really go out with, but it's just the principle of the thing. Well, I am going to go off this medicine tonight because I'm so bloated everywhere and absolutely miserable all the time. I'm tired, so good night. I love you, Lord!

Eden graduated from high school soon after the county competition and proceeded to the state pageant. She was prepared for all areas of the competition; unfortunately she still had not been able to lose the amount of weight that her advisors had requested. Eden was one of the youngest participants at the age of eighteen, and it was her first time attending, so she was learning how the pageant operated. She sat backstage and observed everyone and everything. To her, it all seemed so fabricated. The other contestants were like walking Barbie dolls, or clones, relentlessly scrutinizing their competitors. Each girl would stare endlessly into the mirror, fixing her hair, eye makeup, and clothing—never moving away from her reflection until everything seemed absolutely flawless.

From Eden's perspective, they were all so skinny and had beautiful, flawless skin. "I'm not skinny and definitely don't have pretty skin," Eden mumbled to herself. She was really uncomfortable and didn't feel as though she belonged there. Then she recalled the night she was crowned and that she was chosen to represent her county just like every other contestant. Eden realized how extremely honored she was to be given this opportunity and understood that this was probably a once-in-a-lifetime event for her. She was going to make the best of it and give God the glory.

During her personal panel interview, she was asked about a media incident involving a television evangelist. She thought it was because the panel of judges was aware that she was raised in a Christian home and her father was in the ministry. Eden was thrilled the judges were focusing on subject matters familiar to her and things that were close to her heart. There were several women and men on the panel. A question was asked by a male judge, "Do you believe Jews will go to heaven?"

She answered, "The Bible says that, 'Whosoever shall call upon the name of the Lord shall be saved.'" The judge sat quietly looking at Eden. Eden smiled, sat up straight, and was ready for the next question. Several questions enabled her to quote scripture as a part of her answer. She was feeling blessed and pondered the thought that perhaps she was in the competition for no other reason than to be a Christian witness for her Lord and Savior. For a few moments, she felt that God had chosen to use her in a way she never would have thought possible. When the pageant was over, she saw many young females storming out, sobbing, angrily ranting, and throwing their things. The crown and title was all that mattered to them. Although Eden did not win anything during this competition, she soon realized that the crown she did wear was a tremendous blessing. She finished her one-year reign and passed on her title to the next contestant, forever treasuring her remarkable opportunity.

Eden had been accepted to a college further north where she began her college studies in interior design. She was very excited and ready for the new chapter in her life. She had already auditioned for the a cappella choir in the spring and made it. After starting classes, she found a part-time job on campus. Her roommate and dorm friends all became very close friends. In fact, the girl that lived across the hall from her was one of her best friends from the West Coast! Her world seemed smaller, especially when she had lived and traveled all over the United States! She went through sorority rush week and got involved in everything. She was thriving as a student and enjoying her college life.

Still struggling with her weight and the mysterious medical condition, she wondered if her appearance was the reason no one ever asked her out on a date. She always had many male friends but never dated any of them. In fact, she chose male companions over female. Eden seemed to be able to communicate with males easier than females. Unfortunately, Eden began to connect with some guys in school that did not know the Lord—athletes and directors of the college football team. For some reason, she felt the need, or obligation, to lead them to Christ or "improve their choices." She never chose to follow in their ways but exhausted herself in trying to improve their lifestyle. Eden thought if they could just see Christ's love in her, they would convert. The guys would promise to go to church with her on Sundays, so every Sunday morning, she knocked on their doors, but they never answered. She continued this ritual every Sunday until she left college.

Eden ate lunch with these male friends every day. They would also call her "puffy," a word that had haunted her since high school. They told her she needed to work out more and change her eating habits. What they didn't realize is that she had already been restricting her diet, and she had always exercised. However, she began to modify even more (with no results) in her continual efforts to please them. Eden invested so much time and effort into people that gave her so little in return, and it was an unhealthy, undermining choice she chose to live with.

She was passing all of her courses and maintaining a full schedule as she continued to work part-time. Unfortunately, during Eden's junior year of college, the school informed her that, because the degree she had chosen was such a new program, it was not yet accredited. Needless to say, Eden and the students enrolled in the program were very disturbed with the news. She felt lost about which direction to go in and what to do. She did not want to spend another year at a private school, with her parents paying for her education and not graduating with an accredited degree. It was a very confusing time for her and left her with some difficult decisions to make.

October 18, 1989
Dear Diary,

I have had so much to do and think about! I'm in the horrible process of changing my major to nutrition/dietetics with a minor in exercise physiology. Yes, I'll be here forever. I really am having a horrible time trying to decide what I am going to do! All I want to do is marry a preacher, have kids, and travel. Just like Mom. I need a degree, however. I'm so scared. God, help!

Her medical condition had worsened with uncontrollable hot flashes. Copious amounts of sweat would suddenly, without warning, begin to drip down her face and body onto the floor. It was starting to interfere with her social life and concentration during school. Through this change in her degree program, she felt as though God was giving her an opportunity to leave and maybe get some medical help for her condition. While Eden was away at college, her parents moved back to the Midwest. So she decided to take a semester off and move back in with her parents. She was not looking forward to the move. Eden didn't have the best childhood memories of living in the Midwest, but her plans were to move and stay just long enough to decide what direction she needed to take in regards to her education.

Eden moved in with her parents, knowing it would be quite an adjustment after living on her own for a couple of years. Her parents became more concerned about the progression of her mysterious medical condition. She had already seen several doctors. In the past, a family doctor had even accused her of using drugs because of her erratic behavior, suggesting that she was going down the wrong path because her dad was a missionary. That was disheartening, to say the least. Her faith in doctors was almost nonexistent. She had seen so many of them, and no one knew how to help her. The same blood tests had been repeated several times, and nothing was abnormal. Eden understood that to a doctor or a bystander, her symptoms had to be caused by an outside source, but she knew she was not in control of what was happening, and it only made things more frustrating.

December 21, 1989
Dear Diary,

And now what? So, if I finish school, then what? I graduate with a degree, live with my parents till who knows when. Do I go back to those I started school with or stay by myself? God, why do you seem close yet so far away? Why won't you reveal something to me? You always provide for all my needs, but I need You emotionally right now! I need an answer of some sort. Will You give me someone who I will want to love and serve? I want security in a male. Why? I do not know! Please, Lord, send me a young preacher, single, kind, and yes, handsome ... ha. I love you, Lord, and I want to do your work forever!

December 31, 1989
Dear Diary,

I am very frustrated because of my face. It is full of cystic acne. I went to the doctor, and they said my hormones were fine—then something else is wrong. It's so gross! Who wants to talk to someone with oozing, puffy scabs on his or her face? We definitely do not have the money to keep searching for help! Please help, Lord!

Eden's grandmother had read an article about a young girl who had the same symptoms she was experiencing, and the girl was voicing extreme frustration with her father, a family physician, for not believing her. So Eden made an appointment to see an endocrinologist and took the article with her. The doctor ran some blood tests, more extensive than in the past. The results were positive this time, and he found that she had overactive adrenal glands, due to high levels of the hormone cortisol. Today it is referred to as Cushing's syndrome. Symptoms include obesity, "moon face," mood disorders, facial hair growth, cystic acne, and more. Eden was elated that she finally was given an answer! She wasn't crazy! She really had a disorder, and all she needed was the appropriate treatment. She was given medication for her condition and lost over thirty pounds of water weight in two weeks! Her facial acne started to clear, and emotionally she began to feel more stable. She could not believe that finally things were turning around for her! After all those years of name-calling, Eden longed to confront those who called her "puffy." Oh, how she wished they could see her now! She was so excited about the "new me." But now what? Going back to college was not an option at this point, so she had to find a part-time job at the mall and start some classes at the local community college. Although she looked and felt better physically, she was feeling like a fish out of water, because the plans for her future appeared to be slowly unraveling. She had planned to graduate the following year and dreamed of falling in love and marrying someone who was in the ministry. She wanted children and a Godly husband. She assumed that God was going to bring these dreams to reality, just as He had done for her parents and other family members. She thought she would follow in the same footsteps. Life in the ministry—it was the only life she knew.

Chapter 4

A Wall and Plastic Flowers

Eden and her parents lived in a large Tudor home that overlooked beautiful snowcapped mountains. She was not a proficient skier but enjoyed the mountains and casual skiing. They were members of a small local church, one they had attended in previous years. Eden joined the singles group and the adult choir, where she soon became a routine soloist. There were only a few young people her age, but they all became close friends and frequently spent time together. Once again, Eden had to adjust to the midwestern way and their mannerisms. Having moved from the Deep South, people hugged each other and said "ma'am," "sir," "sweetie," "bless you, honey," and "hey" versus "hi." It was common for people in the midwestern culture to be offended by these displays of affection.

Eden still had plans to return to the college she had previously attended, but during her stay with her parents, she decided it would be best to enroll part-time in the local community college to continue her education. She missed her friends and was quite surprised that she hadn't heard from any of them since she moved. Eden missed having her own space and the freedom of living on her own. She knew her parents were accustomed to their own space as well. Continuous adjustments were needed to coexist, and she was unsure of what the next chapter in her life would bring, but a change was going to be necessary. She scheduled several job interviews and quickly found a part-time job, which enabled her to earn some income as well as a little more independence.

April 13, 1990
Dear Diary,

It's been quite depressing. I don't know what to major or minor in. I always think I do. Then wham—nope. Wrong again. I'm also feeling very lonesome. I miss the beach! I miss my friends, but I don't want to go to my school again. I don't know. I'd give the world if someone would come see me, or call, or at least write. I don't know why people promise to call or write—they lie!

Eden enjoyed her new job and the small group of friends she had met at her church. She became very active with visitation, choir, and Sunday school, with several opportunities to sing in her church and churches in the surrounding area. Sometimes Eden would travel with her parents to other states, and she was frequently asked to sing before her father preached. Even though Eden enjoyed singing, her nerves overwhelmed her at times, but as she became older, the tendency to make mistakes during her songs became less frequent. Once again, Eden was asked to sing at the State Youth Evangelism Conference. It was one of the larger events held within the area, and she knew it was an honor to have been asked to sing for the convention. She would be sharing the stage with several well-known music artists, and she was determined to be well prepared. Her biggest fear was a reoccurrence of the situation that happened last time she sang at a youth conference. Her greatest consolation was that no matter what happened, God could use anything for His glory.

The youth conference arrived quickly, but Eden was ready,

confident, and prepared. The weekend conference went very well, and Eden had a great time meeting the other music artists as well as other young adults from around the state. God had blessed her that weekend by restoring her self-confidence and belief in her abilities to minister to people through music. She sang beautifully, without any mistakes in her music! When the service was over, a man introduced himself to her as Mr. Davidson. He told her about himself and his family and then asked Eden if she would be interested in meeting his son, Heath. After speaking with him for quite some time, she reluctantly gave him her phone number and granted him permission for Heath to call her. She didn't give much thought to their conversation, until a few weeks later when she received a call from Heath.

Eden and Heath had several conversations on the phone prior to meeting but finally decided it was time to meet each other face-to-face. They lived several miles away from each other, and they had not made any special plans for their first date. He was just going to come over to her house so that he could meet her and her parents. When the doorbell rang, she became very anxious. What if she wasn't attracted to him? She was going to feel bad if he drove an hour to her house and she wasn't interested. Eden slowly opened the door—and there he stood, tall, dark and handsome! It was love at first sight! *This only happens in the movies,* she thought excitedly. Nervously, she invited him inside, and they sat on the couch in the living room. They connected immediately and talked until three in the morning. Eden could not believe she had met someone, and of all places, in the Midwest, the place she disliked the most!

They began dating, travelling to see each other every weekend. Their relationship flourished quickly. Eden developed a wonderful relationship with his entire family. Everything seemed to be perfect! Communication was never a problem for them, and they were very comfortable around each other. They could relax and be themselves. She discovered that Heath could also sing! He had a beautiful voice but had never been given the opportunity to sing anywhere. He had only sung with his family in their small church and living room, so when he heard Eden sing, it changed everything. It was as though a challenge had been set before him to do more with his voice. So Heath and Eden began singing together and eventually started travelling to other churches for singing engagements. Eden knew she had found the man God had for her. He was a hard worker, had a servant's heart, loved the Lord, and treated her so well. She could not have chosen anyone better for her. They knew God brought them together, so they were engaged after three months of dating and married six months later. Eden claimed Eph. 5:31–33: "For this reason a man shall leave his father and mother and be joined to his wife, and the two shall become one flesh. This is a great mystery, but I speak concerning Christ and the church. Nevertheless, let each one of you in particular so love his own wife as himself, and let the wife see that she respects her husband."

3-10-91
Dear Diary,

Well, we had one awesome weekend—much better than last! We sang, and it was perfect. Everything is fine. Well, it looks like the wedding will be a lot sooner! He was talking about it! He doesn't want to wait, and I don't either! I love him so much! It just gets harder and very old to go back and forth. So we will see. Thank you, Lord! I love you so very much!

The wedding was held in the church where Eden and her parents were members. Eden had accepted Christ and was baptized in this church when she was six years old. Now at the age of twenty-two, she was getting married in the same church, after being gone for sixteen years. Eden's mother had decorated the church and had taken care of all the details for the wedding. The platform was encircled with gorgeous floral arrangements, draped beautifully over majestic white columns, adorned with white lace and glowing candles. Her father performed the ceremony, and her brother, who also sang beautifully, engaged the audience with his majestic solo. Eden's new husband also sang a song of promise to her. She could not have asked for a more special gift from her new husband. The wedding and the reception were magical, and they were able to leave for their honeymoon in a white limousine. Eden was so excited to start their new life as the wife of a loving husband. They were one!

They soon arrived at their honeymoon location. The suite was beautiful, and she was so excited to share her first night with him—no distractions, no inhibitions. Suddenly, Heath was different. The picture-perfect scene in her dreams became abruptly the opposite of what she had expected. She had waited all of her life for this special night, but for some reason, her new husband seemed preoccupied with everything except her. His disinterest took her by surprise. Was it something she did? She didn't know what to say or what to do. Eden wasn't sure what she was feeling. She began to wonder if this was what their marriage was going to be like, and at the same time, she was feeling guilty for even entertaining those thoughts so soon after the wedding! Was she expecting too much from her new husband? She didn't think so, but she held back her tears and continued to smile. But when the lights went out that evening, she lay awake and just prayed; she prayed she had made the choice God wanted her to make.

When they returned from the honeymoon, they moved into an older house. Their first home was a brick ranch, probably built in the 1970s. The house had three bedrooms, two bathrooms, and a large living room with an old wood stove in the corner. The kitchen was in the front of the house with a door leading to the carport. A sliding glass door led to a very large backyard with a swing set and fence that was draped with a grapevine. She could smell the grapes from the backdoor. The kitchen had a large double window facing the driveway. Eden would sit and eat breakfast every morning and gaze at the large fir tree in the front yard. There were cinderblocks dividing their driveway and the neighbor's. Of particular interest to her were the fake, plastic flowers her neighbor had planted inside the cinder blocks. Who plants plastic flowers? One thing was certain; they were always colorful, remained in constant bloom, and could withstand all extremes of nature. It was quite unrealistic and actually somewhat annoying. Sometimes she imagined quietly removing them and replacing them with real flowers. She just had to laugh.

Eden was unable to find work. She started her mornings with prayer and personal Bible study. After her quiet time, she went to aerobic classes at the local hospital. After lunch, she usually spent the afternoon cleaning or doing household chores. She had the cleanest house in town! Heath went to work at four in the morning and didn't come home till after four in the afternoon. She always tried to have dinner ready for him as soon as he came through the door. Her mom had always done that for her dad when he came home. She wanted to do the same for her husband. Eden thought it was respectful since he had been at work all day and she had been at home. She wanted to be a "good" wife. They never had much time together in the evenings because he had to go to bed around eight. She was lonely most of the day and longed to see her husband and spend time with him. He was always tired, and she understood. He also worked another job on the weekends, construction, which frequently required traveling out of town. He didn't really need to, but he had always loved working, traveling, and making extra money. It was enjoyable to him. Eden thought the extra income was a bonus, and he invited her to travel with him, but she was never comfortable going with him. She didn't like the atmosphere of his work. Even so, sometimes she would join him just so she would not be left alone.

Eden longed for Christian fellowship with couples their age. She wanted the chance to serve in a larger church again. So she began to earnestly pray during her morning Bible study that God would move them to a place where they would have more opportunities, somewhere they could grow as a Christian couple. Eden and Heath were currently the only young couple in their church. She wanted friendships and quality time with her husband, and she had a strong desire for spiritual growth. If they were to have children anytime in the near future, she really did not want to raise them in the small anti-Christian community where they currently lived. Most of the people had religious beliefs that were very foreign to her. She remembered her childhood days, attending school in this area, and it was very difficult if you were not raised according to the views of this community. She was always considered an outcast. As she thought about her future and the desire to have children, she had a bigger vision for her family than what this town had to offer. She was hoping God would use them in a much larger capacity. She wanted Heath to have more opportunities, and she prayed that God would use him in ways that he had never imagined.

Eden decided to enroll in college classes to continue her education, but she still could not find employment. To get an application for any position in town, she had to pass a typing test and take an aptitude test (GATB). She took the typing test five times! She could not type well; therefore, she was not given the opportunity to start an application process. Needless to say, it was very frustrating, and she thought it was an unjust system. The employment service told Eden she could substitute teach in the school system, so she agreed to the position and took whatever days they offered. The early morning calls and unknown destinations became unnerving to her at times, but overall it was a rewarding job and good experience.

October 10, 1991
Dear Diary,

It's our two-month anniversary already. He is golfing—again. I swear it's an obsession. Oh well, we all have them, right? My GATB scores were fine. No job yet. I did substitute for a high school ceramic/sculpture class. It was hard but extra money. I am so tired of sitting at home! This is the dumbest, smallest town I have ever lived in. I have no friends, no job, nothing to do, no one to talk to. My husband is out playing golf with his friends. I don't think he'd really understand. I pray every day that we will move and find friends, a good church, and I can find a job. God won't allow me to be miserable and lonely, will He? Well, at least we have a good marriage! Thank you, God, for him!

Eden's opportunities to sing became more frequent, and this involved some travelling. She had been asked to sing for a conference held at a church she and her brother had attended when they were teenagers. While attending the conference, Eden's brother asked her to sing a duet with him; he had actually written the song they would sing and record on his next CD. Eden was given the music to learn, and in a few weeks, she would fly to the recording studio to record the duet. She was honored and elated to have this opportunity. It would be the first time recording in a studio! There wasn't much time to prepare, but she wanted it to be perfect.

Meanwhile, Eden and Heath's first Christmas was spent with both families, and it was very enjoyable. Eden was busy with substitute teaching, high school, junior high, and elementary school. She had enrolled in another semester of school, and everything was going well, despite her secret desire to move. Little did she know that her world was about to change.

Heath came home from work one afternoon and told her that he was going to lose his job in a few weeks. Obviously, she was nervous yet excited, feeling that God had answered her prayers! She also felt very guilty. She had prayed for God to move them to another location, but now Heath was going to lose his job. *Be careful what you pray for,* she thought to herself. She knew, however, that this was going to be the only way her husband would leave this town. She was certain this was an answer to her prayers, but she couldn't help but feel responsible and somewhat nervous about their future. Questions started flooding her head: Where do we go from here? What if Heath doesn't want to move? What will he do? How will we pay our bills?

January 23, 1992
Dear Diary,

He could lose his job any day now! Not another job yet! Not even promising! In fact, he hasn't even been looking. I'm scared. I'm spiritually D.E.A.D.! No question about it. Signed, Help!

The day finally arrived, and Heath was officially unemployed. Eden continued her classes and occasionally did substitute teaching. The burden of losing a job created a very stressful atmosphere between them. For the first time, she and Heath began to argue about finances, job opportunities, and moving choices. Eden was anxious about the possibility of staying in the same town indefinitely. They came to an agreement that they would try to sell their house. A short time later, Heath was offered the opportunity to work full-time for the construction company he had previously worked for on the weekends. This required him to be gone for several days at a time. Needless to say, this made matters worse for her.

February 18, 1992
Dear Diary,

I'm very frustrated and depressed but also excited. First of all, he was gone on our first Valentine's Day. He did send me six beautiful roses. He will be back next Tuesday or so. I hate this! It's so quiet it's incredible! I hate quiet! But I am excited because we are going to be gone March 18–25 so I can record the duet with my brother! I am so excited! Good night.

Eden was hurt when their first Valentine's Day passed, and Heath wasn't home. There were six roses in a vase on her kitchen table. She sat there alone, staring at them, wishing she was not alone on that special day. However, every day was the same—lonely. She was always alone! As she stood in the kitchen, she glanced past the roses on the table, and her eyes were drawn to her neighbor's plastic flowers, just outside her front window. She couldn't help but think, *My flowers are going to die before my husband even gets home.* Heath would be gone all week; he only came home on the weekends. When Heath did come home, he would scold her about everything. She couldn't do anything right anymore! The kitchen sink was never shiny enough; the clothes were never ironed correctly; the checkbook was never correct; the rims on the car were too dirty; the clothes were left in the dryer and needed to be folded and put away. You name it. There was always something out of place or not done right. She thought he was just stressed or tired. Eden was stressed and tired too! She thought she was doing a good job as a wife and homemaker. She had plenty of time to clean, so how could she not perfect the skill? As she stroked the wilting petal of her roses, she realized her spirit was dwindling as well. "Beautiful roses have no more value than plastic flowers if the love behind them isn't real," she mumbled to herself.

February 25, 1992
Dear Diary,

He amazes me. He spent $200 on a watch and shoes, and I feel guilty for buying hairspray! He's rewarding himself. Well what do I have to do to "reward" myself? Just because I don't work. Everyone needs rewards no matter what they do or don't do! Where and when do you put a limit on it? He has been nagging me every time he comes home: my driving, cleaning, checkbook, money, and so on. I am tired of it. He never tells me I'm pretty anymore. I don't guess I am. If he only understood how I feel about my stupid face and body. Bye. Signed, Angry and Depressed

They were finally able to sell their house, and the buyers asked if they could move in within twenty-four hours. Heath was working out of town, so Eden had to pack and move everything without his help. "I have done this more than once," she laughed to herself. She packed up the entire house and put everything in storage, minus the two suitcases that held the clothes they needed for the next few weeks. It was definitely not as easy as she thought it would be. They had to move in with his parents for a week while Eden finished the school semester.

The semester had come to an end, and it was time for Eden and Heath to fly out to meet her brother to record the duet. She was excited about this experience but also anxious to visit her old college town. As Eden sat on the plane, she suddenly became very ill. Just three weeks prior to the trip, her doctor had prescribed some new medication, and she was having a bad reaction. She later found out the dosage was too strong, but she was very sick the entire flight. To make the trip more interesting, the elderly man sitting in the seat in front of them died during flight! Eden had been making frequent trips to the lavatory, but she was now unable to move from her seat because the staff had laid the man on the floor in front of the lavatories to perform CPR. It was a very memorable flight to say the least. The plane finally landed, and she was still not feeling well, but she had to go straight to the studio and rehearse the duet with her brother. She could not believe her first opportunity to record in a studio had finally arrived, and she felt horrible. The time in the recording studio proved to be an awesome educational experience and a special time that she would never forget.

During their stay with Eden's brother, she and Heath were able to visit with many of her college friends. They also began reevaluating their situation and discussed various options they might have. Heath needed a better job, and they realized they were visiting an area that had more churches, more job opportunities, great schools, and close Christian friends. So they began to search for available places to live and soon found a great price on an apartment. The apartments were located down the street from one of the newest, fastest-growing churches in the area. Eden was extremely excited! God had answered her prayer, down to the smallest of details! Eden and Heath flew back home and started making plans to move—completely by faith, praying the Lord would continue to provide for all their needs. They said good-bye to their families and moved to the South the following week.

The move went very well, and they both had jobs within the first two weeks. Eden started work as an assistant in a doctor's office, and Heath started working for a local construction company that, unfortunately, still required him to travel. They joined the large church down the street and became actively involved in the music program as well as the couples Sunday school class. They were enjoying the church fellowship, the preaching, their jobs, and their new apartment. Eden's only concern was Heath's work hours … again! He had to work very long hours and was constantly travelling between two states. It was a schedule that was all too familiar to her.

May 18, 1992
Dear Diary,

Not too much has happened. We've been working long hours. Especially Heath. We both hate his hours, and we miss each other during the weekdays. Nights (and weekends) are harder. We seem to get upset if the littlest thing is said. We're working on it. Just going through a tough time, I guess. Well, thank you, Lord. Good night.

Nine days before their first year anniversary, Eden had a wonderful surprise—she was pregnant! She was extremely excited, nervous, and shocked but definitely not prepared. She and heath were still in the ninety-day waiting period for health insurance with their new jobs. This was going to be another financial burden for them. How were they going to pay for a pregnancy? She was just so thankful God had answered her prayer by making a way for them to move to a place that was suitable for raising their little boy or girl! Eden hoped Heath would be excited too. She wanted to wait and tell Heath the surprising news on their first anniversary.

August 10, 1992—written on a Zofran sticky note:

Have a wonderful day honey. I love you and look forward to many years with you and our new gift of life from God.
Happy first anniversary!
See you soon.
Love, Your Hubby

August 11, 1992
Dear Diary,

Well, you like my anniversary card? I was very surprised, but oh well, can't wait to see next year's note. I actually lied to people about our anniversary so I wouldn't be embarrassed. Pretty sad! He's gone again tonight. You know? He never tells me I'm pretty or, better yet, beautiful anymore. He used to tell me all the time when we dated. Oh well, I'm "fine" nowadays. I feel awful and I know I look it too! I know he thinks so! I know he does, and I don't know what to do!

Eden shared her pregnancy news with Heath over the phone. It was not what she had planned, especially when it was her first child. No more roses. She would have settled for plastic flowers from her neighbor's yard! She had to admit it hurt when her husband didn't think she was worth more than a sticky note! Eden didn't expect much, but she was definitely not expecting a sticky note. She was beginning to wonder if he really, truly loved her. *What are his true feelings for me? This was our first anniversary!* she thought as confusion and disappointment consumed her. *This should have been a very special day. We didn't have to spend a lot of money, but it could have been romantic and meaningful. He wasn't even there!* Nothing! She began to cry. Eden was hurt and, yes, angry. She never would have thought her marriage would be like this.

She was very ill with the pregnancy, but God was providing for their every need. In fact, the church paid their medical bills in full. It was a miracle! Eden was humbled at such a gift. The baby was healthy, and they soon found out they were having a precious little boy! She found that it was difficult not living close to her parents. It would have been fun sharing this first-time experience with them. She knew what she gave up by moving farther away, and her parents understood why. The baby was due in the spring, and they were living in a one-bedroom apartment. They had been looking for a larger unit, but nothing was available, so the baby's crib would need to be in the dining room temporarily. Eden was just excited for her new little man to come into the world. She knew he didn't care where he slept; he was going to be loved and taken care of.

February 17, 1993
Dear Diary,

Things are rough right now! Valentine's weekend and day sucked! We fought (bad). Friday and especially Saturday. Then Sunday we spent the day together, but he didn't even get me a card for Valentine's Day! Needless to say, I was extremely shocked. This is becoming a regular occurrence. He never touches me. I'm tired of this I could die. I don't know what to do. I'm so miserable I could scream.

Eden was really starting to question her marriage, herself, her decisions, and even God. She knew she had prayed about every decision she had made, so why was everything backfiring? She was building a wall of protection between Heath and herself. She was slowly becoming defensive and angry due to the neglect and fighting. As a child, when she was "the new kid," she would sit quietly and listen to others talk about her. Eden wished she had stood up for herself! Instead, she harbored resentful feelings that developed into unhealthy emotions. Now that Eden was married, she didn't want to be bullied; nor did she want to be ignored or neglected. On special occasions, she always gave Heath cards, served candlelight dinners, or at least gave him a small gift. Was she not worth the same treatment? She didn't understand what she was doing wrong, but she noticed that she was in a constant state of anger and confusion.

Eden's brother had started his own company located within a few miles of the church. She decided to resign from the doctor's office and go to work for him, so that when her baby was born, she could take him to work with her. The church members were so kind to Eden and Heath and hosted several baby showers for them. They were blessed beyond measure, lacking nothing for the baby. Heath worked the nightshift six days a week. He was never home, and she was fearful of him not being home when the baby was born. So Eden had her mom flown in to help for a short period.

In the spring of 1993, Eden requested that labor be induced so that Heath could be with her when their baby boy was born. They named him James Davidson. At birth, he was very healthy, for which they were thankful. However, when they brought their precious little boy home, he cried all night. Eden's little gift never slept—night or day! He was the cutest little baby, but he kept them up all day and all night. This change of lifestyle began to turn their world upside down, and just two weeks after James was born, Heath was involved in a horrible car accident.

May 5, 1993
Dear Diary,

Well, yesterday morning I was in the hospital all day. Yes, two days ago, I was up with James from 4:30 to 6:30 a.m. I was expecting Heath home around 6:00 am. I got a scary phone call at 6:30 a.m. from the emergency room. Heath had fallen asleep at the wheel of his car. My brother and friends took me to the hospital. He looked awful. He had shattered his left leg, had a huge black eye, swollen bloody nose, and had cuts with blood everywhere! I freaked! He went into surgery to put plates and screws in his leg. The surgeon said he shouldn't even be alive. That's all I could think about! Anyway, he has been out of it for two days. Yesterday, I had been up since 2:30 a.m. with James, and again today since 4:30. I'm so exhausted I'm almost sick to my stomach. Well, I'm glad I still have my wonderful husband! Thank you, Lord, for everything!

For eight days, Eden had to stay in a motel, one state away, with her newborn baby. She continuously paced the floor to get James to go to sleep and stop crying. She would have given anything for someone to have come and help her, pray with her, or just hug her.

It was an exhausting and scary eight days. She was excited when Heath was finally released from the hospital and they could go back home. They were still in a one-bedroom apartment, so she had placed James's crib and changing table in the dining room. She had no other choice, but it worked out fine. As a result, the dining table had to be moved behind the couch in the living room. It really was crowded. Now, there was a hospital bed for Heath next to the wall in front of the couch. However, they couldn't afford a two-bedroom apartment, so they would have to utilize the space they had. To complicate matters, Heath's work accident resulted in a 60 percent decrease in income. Through it all, God blessed them, and they knew He was protecting them.

Some of their family came to visit them for a few days, and it was helpful to have assistance with preparing meals and caring for the baby. Even so, having a lot of people in such a small place became stressful. A nurse came every other day to check on Heath. Heath couldn't walk, bathe himself, or do anything without Eden's assistance. She had a newborn and a husband, both totally dependent on her for everything! She didn't know how to take care of either of them very well. She often felt that she needed someone to take care of her, even if it was just for a small amount of time. Everything became overwhelming very quickly.

June 26, 1993
Dear Diary,

Well, things are back to their ugly self again. We aren't getting along. I feel so far from him emotionally that I can't be physical. It worries me and scares me. I try not to put my son first, but emotionally I guess I am more attached. I never thought I'd have this problem. It's not small either! My son laughed for the first time today. That was so sweet. It is 10:06 p.m., and he's on the bed with him, and I'm in the bathroom. We just had another fight. I don't even want to go in there. We have no space (except the toilet). My attitude stinks, I know, but I'm not sure how to change it. I'm not sure what's wrong. He is in there singing. That makes me so angry. He always talks to me like I'm a criminal. Then one minute later he's singing or whistling like it was nothing. I don't know what to think about our relationship right now. I want so bad to talk to someone, but I don't want anyone to know. I'm frustrated. I don't want to pray, so I don't. That's my problem, I am sure. Good night. Signed, Frustrated, Mad, and Scared

The bathroom was Eden's safe place where she could lock the door and hide away, sit on the floor, cry, or write in her diary. She could get away from Heath and think. Sometimes she felt like a little girl again, asking herself the same questions. "Why doesn't he like me?" "What is wrong with me?" Now she had this sweet little boy, and she felt that he had been brought into the middle of a very dysfunctional relationship. It grieved her, because he didn't deserve to be in this turmoil. Eden had never heard her parents argue openly, and they seldom disagreed with each other. Why was she having this problem in her home? It didn't seem fair! She was ready to take her son and leave. She started to feel trapped, and the wall between her and Heath was growing higher with each passing day.

Late one afternoon, Eden was sitting on the corner of her bed, staring out the window. She was cradling James in her left arm and covering his little ear with her right hand. It was as if she was in a Charlie Brown special, and she was on the phone listening to "Wawawawawa" at the bedroom door. Heath was standing in the doorway on his crutches, scolding her in his loud, spiteful voice about everything she seemed to be doing wrong. Eden attempted to block his voice out of her head while she tried to shelter her son's ears. She sat motionless and nursed her baby, tears streaming down her face uncontrollably. She wondered when her husband's deluge of critical words was going to stop … and if her life was ever going to change.

Ironically, her neighbor's cinderblock wall of plastic flowers represented her life perfectly. Each day, the wall between her and Heath was getting taller. Her life seemed to be an identical replica of those silly plastic flowers. They were pretty on the outside but completely artificial. Eden was just trying to get through each day, and nothing felt real anymore. She would put on a smile, go to church, and sing, greet people, and be social. She wasn't intentionally trying to be a dishonest person, but she was hiding an embarrassing, unexplainable situation. Would anyone believe her if she told anyone what was going on? She doubted it. Instead of seeking help, she kept everything inside, resulting in constant nausea and such tightness in her stomach. Eating became very difficult, sometimes impossible. Heath's constant comments of how much Eden was eating and his "pig" remarks when she finally did eat began to take a toll on her. She already had a long history of struggling with weight loss and her overall appearance. Eating became the only thing in her life she could control ... and that's exactly what she did!

July 9, 1993
Dear Diary,

I don't even know who I married, and I'm actually wondering what I fell in love with. I'm sorry, but everything I do, he harps on me, and everything I don't do, he harps on me. He is just so downright rude and spiteful! I don't want to hug him, kiss him, or touch him. He cracks stupid, mean jokes; he makes me feel an inch high when it comes to my son, cooking, work, him, and everything. He gets upset when I don't jump and do something right then. If I leave something on the floor, he kicks it or yells at me. I do not know what to do! Signed, PO-ed

Due to the accident, Heath was out of work for almost a year, and they were unsure of what was going to happen next. Eden was still working for her brother, but she was beginning to wonder if moving there had been a mistake. Perhaps she had prayed for the wrong thing. Did she assume too quickly that this was God's will for them? She was so confused and frustrated, she wasn't sure what to think. She was struggling spiritually, and angry because no one from the church had come to visit or pray with them after the accident. It made no sense! Eden and Heath had been very active in church activities and were very visible due to their involvement as soloists in the music program. They were just down the street! Didn't it occur to anyone that they might need some encouragement? Eden just wanted a hug, a prayer, some affirmation that life would get better! She wanted them to care! She was quickly losing faith in her so-called Christian friends. A few months passed before Heath was able to go back to church. When they did attend, it was very difficult for Eden to worship. Truthfully, she was bitter and hurt. The people around her had not lifted a finger to befriend her during these difficult times, but they called themselves Christians. Really?

The next few months, she and Heath traveled back and forth from the hospital for follow-up appointments and also a second surgery on Heath's leg. After many long weeks of treatment, Heath was released to start physical therapy. Heath was finally on his way to recovery. Later, when Heath was released to go back to work, they had to make another decision about employment. Eden no longer worked for her brother because he relocated to another state. She and Heath desperately wanted a fresh start, so once again, they began considering the possibility of moving to a different location, perhaps even a different state. By now, Eden was apprehensive about praying for anything. Her track record caused her to question her own decisions. She seriously doubted her ability to pray and actually "hear" what God was saying.

Eden received a phone call from her brother, letting her know that the two of them had been asked to sing a duet at the church where they had attended high school. It had been years since she had seen her closest friends whose lives had always influenced her in such positive ways. She was excited about showing James to all of them. This church was located in Eden's favorite place—she liked this town better than any other. What wonderful memories she had! She loved the church, the beach, and the people. She began to dream about living there again. She believed it would be good for their marriage, and it was certainly a great place to raise their son!

While they were visiting, Heath fell in love with it as well, and since they had some connections, Heath began to look for employment. Heath interviewed with a company that was located just outside of the city, and he was promised a job! Everything seemed to be falling into place! Their second anniversary was a few days away, and James was only three months old. Eden was eager for a change and a new beginning. She was convinced that being a part of this specific church would be beneficial for Heath and her and would surely be a great place for James to grow up.

In Eden's diary, at the bottom of the page, these words were written: "Life's challenges should be viewed not as stumbling blocks but as building blocks as faith." She was hoping one day her walls of defense would come down so she could rebuild a wall of solid faith.

March 28, 1994
Dear Diary,

My precious son, James, will be one year in three weeks! He's a big boy! Then we move April 16 to the beach. It looks like Heath will have a good job. He was released from rehab. He has been out of work for eleven months! I'm nervous and hope he does okay. But I am glad. I'm still thin but better. I was nauseated a few days; now I'm better. Well, see ya! "Better"

April 17, 1994
Dear Diary,

Well, I've been very busy! Last week, my husband's parents came and helped us move. We moved on my James's first birthday. It was crazy. I felt so bad. We moved out late afternoon, so we had to go out to eat, to the creamery, and had a candle put into a scoop of ice scream. We had the girls behind the counter videotape all of us singing to him. He just roamed around. He didn't eat. The next day, we drove to Heath's interview. It went really well. We have to wait till Monday to see if he got the job. This is really scary! We moved into our new apartment. Our rent is higher. Oh well. I am feeling much better about being here. Bye.

It did not take long before Eden's new building blocks of faith started crumbling. Life quickly consumed every inch of her soul. Heath did not get the job he had been promised. He had gone through the final interviewing process on their move down, and after they moved in a week later, he received devastating news. The company had decided not to hire him, due to his previous involvement in an accident while he was on the job. Eden didn't understand. The company was aware of his accident prior to the final interview, so they could have notified him before they moved. By now, they were in dire need of financial help. Rent was due in a week, along with other bills. Nothing seemed to go right for them anymore. She began to question God. Her prayer life was almost nonexistent, and she had lost the ability to understand God's will and direction for her life. Stress was eating away at her—mentally, spiritually, and physically. How were they going to handle another job loss, another roadblock, and another strain on their marriage?

May 4, 1994
Dear Diary,

I'm so depressed right now I could literally take my life. If it wasn't for my son, it's hard to explain. He still doesn't have a job yet. He's turned down a couple; the rest have turned him down. All he looks for is the same type of job, and it is ruining our marriage. If my son wasn't here, I think we would split. Our marriage sucks! There's nothing that will help it either. We hate each other! There's no love! There hasn't been in a long time. He is gone with my son right now, who knows where. I know for sure it's not to get roses. Sunday is Mother's Day! He'll forget or do nothing! Signed, Miserable

Weeks went by before Heath found work. Eden had not finished school, so she really did not have anything to offer the work force that would equal the cost of daycare. She was blessed to stay home and take care of James. She knew the Lord had a plan for them to be where they were. She was praying that God was going to heal their marriage. She loved living in this town. It was her favorite place to live, and she knew they were going to have plenty of Christian couples to go out with. They joined the large church Eden had attended when she was in high school, and she was eager to become actively involved again.

After long months of waiting, they received a financial settlement from Heath's accident. A few months later, they were able to purchase a small patio home. Things were somewhat better for Eden, and her renewed faith was beginning to grow. Getting involved in the church and rekindling old friendships was exactly what Eden needed. Heath, however, remained unchanged. In fact, Heath became jealous of the friendships and relationships she had rekindled. It was as though he resented her for having lived there years ago, and instead of sharing the excitement with her, he seemed to grow increasingly angry. Eden couldn't win! She still couldn't please him.

They were going to celebrate their third anniversary. In three years, they had moved four times already, endured two job losses, survived a major accident, had a child ... and they were struggling! She wasn't sure if Heath no longer loved her or if the stress of their circumstances was just getting in the way of a healthy marriage. On their third anniversary, Heath sent Eden three roses in a vase, but, as usual, he was not home to celebrate. In their three years of marriage, nothing had changed ... except the view outside her window.

>My roses are red.
>My violets are blue.
>The roses you sent me,
>They wilt and fade quickly.
>The blooms in the vase
>Die ere you see my face.
>The rose that is plastic,
>The violet that's fake,
>Stands sturdy and tall
>In a cinderblock wall,
>Forever its bloom for beauty's sake,
>Symbolic of life, as if a mistake.
>
>—Eden

Chapter 5

Actions Speak Louder Than Words ... Or Do They?

E<small>DEN WAS SITTING IN</small> the front row of one of the largest churches in America. Her heart was beating so hard she thought it was going to jump out of her chest. It had been years since she had sung in front of so many people. She was actively involved in this same church back in high school and absolutely loved it. A lot had changed since then. She was no longer the teenager who sang solos on their stage and sang in their youth choir. She was now a wife and a mother, hiding behind a fake smile that masked the distress of her secret life at home. Eden was extremely honored, however, to have been asked to sing for the morning service. She was hoping this would be the beginning of a new chapter in her life, and she wanted to take every opportunity God gave her to minister to others through song.

Eden eagerly became involved in Sunday school and the adult choir. She was soon asked to teach first-grade choir, composed of about ninety children. She wasn't sure about taking on such a daunting task, but she had a hard time saying no to others' requests. In addition to this new responsibility, she frequently sang for banquets, Sunday school assemblies, youth events, morning and evening services, holiday programs, and more. She quickly became overwhelmed with so much going on. She and Heath also sang together sometimes, even though their relationship continued to struggle. Eden did not understand why. She believed the reason he talked down to her and treated her disrespectfully was related to the high levels of stress in their lives. But even when the stress would ease, he seemed to remain the same, sometimes even worse! There were no identifiable reasons behind his actions or words. His words would cut like a sword! As bad as it may sound, she thought, *I wish he would have hit me and get it over with!* She never could understand why he would say mean, hurtful things to her for no reason. If she didn't have dinner prepared, the laundry finished, the dishes washed and put away correctly, he would be say very spiteful and insulting things to her. If she had more singing engagements than he did, it made him angry and jealous. There was no excuse for it! He would constantly demean her as a Christian woman by using scripture against to make her feel unworthy. *I suppose the Psalms 52 was overlooked*, she thought as she read aloud Psalms 52:1–4, "Why do you boast in evil, O mighty man? The goodness of God endures continually. Your tongue devises destruction, like a sharp razor, working deceitfully. You love evil more than good, lying rather than speaking righteousness. You love all devouring words, you deceitful tongue."

September 24, 1994
Dear Diary,

Well, I was actually having a great day! My husband and I were going to have a fun night, just the two of us (well, three). Then he says something totally from nowhere, and it stabs me in the back! It really hurt my feelings! Then he says, "Truth hurts sometimes." Can you believe that? He is such an inconsiderate—! I was actually feeling like snuggling, not now, not ever. Why did he say something so rude? Now he's trying to apologize! Why? He doesn't mean it! He just wants to get on with our night. He can, but it won't be with me. You know? I really don't think he loves me! I really don't! Not true love anyway. Not unconditionally! Oh well, Hurt! Again!

October 21, 1994
Dear Diary,

I sang two weeks ago in the morning service. I didn't have a voice, but it went fine anyway. I sing again in two weeks. I've been asked for the biggest banquet of the year (1,200 people) and an SS banquet. All three in one weekend. Then I have two SS classes and a Christmas banquet scheduled. Plus I have to prepare for first-grade performances. I'm very overwhelmed but blessed.

"How is God able to use either or us when our home life is a wreck?" Eden would ask herself. The confusion and frustration that flooded her heart each night and day was almost unbearable. She wanted help, but if she told anyone, she was fearful that no one would ask to sing again. She worried that she would be frowned upon if she needed time for counseling or guidance. She felt certain she would be misunderstood for wanting to leave her husband. She continued to smile, and she functioned as if her life was perfect and in order, but it was a vicious cycle. She had done the same thing over and over and over again! She knew exactly what to say and how to act under any circumstance. She had done this her entire life! She wanted to be authentic and genuine, but she was living a lie.

Eden's desire to serve the Lord began to conflict with the deep inner turmoil stirring within her. Singing was her gift and her joy, but she could feel her heart growing cold and hardened. Everything she had put her faith in was collapsing beneath her feet. She began to question God, His people, His church, and everything she had believed about living a Christian life. She had been taught that if she was faithful to Christ and lived her life for Him, she would be blessed. She thought if she stayed pure before marriage, she would be blessed in her marriage; if she prayed about whom she would marry, she would find the right man; and if she committed her marriage to the Lord, divorce would never be an option. If she would just do A, then B would occur, because two plus two always equals four, right? She wasn't intentionally underestimating the power of God, but she really struggled with the "what ifs." Eden honestly thought she had done all the right things, but A did not result in B, and for some reason two plus two was not coming out to four! Did she not follow all the right steps of obedience? Eden was wondering how life could turn upside down regardless of someone's faithfulness. No one prepared her for the unexpected circumstances she had to face! She felt as though she had lost control of everything around her, and she had no idea what was happening with her life. Everything seemed to spiral out of control. She just knew her marriage wasn't right, and she was miserable. She felt misunderstood and abused. She didn't have any physical bruises, but the emotional wounds were deep and painful.

January 10, 1995
Dear Diary,

We sang Sunday. It went really well, I believe. We sing again in a week. However, we can't get along! Do you realize if I leave anything out on the floor, he says things like, "Can't you pick up after yourself? Aren't you adult enough to put something back after you get it?" Can you believe how degrading he is? There are so many other ways he could phrase it without degrading me. Basically, he doesn't love me unconditionally. I'm here, and that's it. He is also upset that my brother and I are singing for a big conference and he isn't.
  Signed, Confused!

Eden was very confused by Heath's insecurity, jealousy, and negative temperament. Their relationship grew progressively worse. Eden was teaching first-grade choir and enjoyed it but sometimes wondered if it was adding to their stress at home. She decided to finish out the year of her commitment to teach and then relinquish the position to another volunteer. She always prayed about where God wanted her to serve and spend her time and energy, but she had become fatigued and weary. There was no joy at home, and teaching became more of a burden than a pleasure.

Eden had a wonderful Christian friend whose young boy was the same age as James. Whenever they could, they would spend time together going to the beach, the playground, and of course frequent gatherings that involved famous fast-food Happy Meals. One particular day, she and her friend Tammy had planned an overnight stay with their boys at Tammy's lake house. They took the canoe out on the water and enjoyed swimming in the lake as the boys played together. It was a full day of fun for all! Eden and Tammy relaxed that evening with a good meal as they watched girlie movies and shared stories. It was a great getaway for the little boys as well as Tammy and Eden. They left the lake the next morning and arrived back at Eden's house around 3:30 p.m. Eden was going to be late for her first-grade choir rehearsal, so she did not have dinner prepared for Heath. She quickly bathed James and began to get ready. Heath came home just as she was leaving for church with James. He was in a foul mood, which was not that unusual. She nervously explained to him that they had just recently arrived home from the lake and she was running late for her choir rehearsal, so she did not have dinner prepared. It was evident that Heath was irritated and upset with her, but there was nothing she could do about it. Unexpectedly, Heath said something to Eden that she would never forget. He looked at her with a blank stare and said, "Why don't you go back to the lake and drown."

Eden was stunned with disbelief. *What in the world did I do to deserve to drown in a lake?* she thought. She wanted to leave him instantly. Again, something inside of her wished he had just hit her in the face! It would not have hurt as much! If he had slapped her and left a bruise, then she would have visible evidence that he was hurting her. But she had nothing to show others to make them believe her. There was certainly no way to prove how deeply he was hurting her on the inside. She hated him for it.

Eden methodically finished getting ready for church and went back into the kitchen where Heath was making a sandwich. Eden slipped off her wedding ring and gave it to Heath, saying, "When you no longer wish I was dead, you can give this back to me." She choked back the tears. Trying to keep her emotions intact, she left the house with James and drove to church. Her heart was aching so much she couldn't breathe. Her entire body shook, and she felt an unusual heaviness that felt like waves of pain. She arrived at the church, not even remembering how she got there. She was numb. Her mind was racing, and she didn't want to move from the car. She was frozen. Church was the last place she wanted to be after what Heath just told her. She wanted to be alone, away from the smiling, happy people. As she sat in the car, it seemed as if she heard her dad say, "It's time to go in." She wanted to scream and hit the steering wheel. She was hurt and angry and needed to cry without holding back, but James was in the car. She had to compose herself, put on a smile, and take her precious, innocent son to the nursery, so she could greet all the people who thought her life was just peachy. She managed to get through choir practice as though her life was normal and she would be going home to a happy, loving husband.

When practice was over, she went to the nursery to get James and began the long drive home. She was extremely nervous, her heart was racing, and her stomach was in knots. She wanted to call someone and ask them if what Heath had said to her was normal. She wondered if she should even return home with James. But whom would she call? She just knew she wanted to go as far away from him as possible. She was afraid, humiliated, and trapped—with no place to go.

That night, she read Psalms 55:1–8, "Give ear to my prayer, O God and do not hide yourself from my supplication. Attend to me, and hear me; I am restless in my complaint, and moan noisily, Because of the voice of the enemy, Because of the oppression of the wicked; for they bring down trouble upon me, and the wrath they hate me. My heart is severely pained within me. And the terrors of death have fallen upon me. Fearfulness and trembling have come upon me, and horror has overwhelmed me. So I said, 'Oh, that I had wings like a dove! I would fly away and be at rest. Indeed, I would wander far off, and remain in the wilderness. I would hasten my escape from the windy storm and tempest.'"

March 11, 1995
Dear Diary,

Gosh, I really wish sometimes I wasn't married! He can be so cruel, spiteful, rude, and absolutely hateful!

Eden's coping techniques and defense mechanisms were becoming unhealthy. The wall of protection she had created was getting taller and thicker. She would *not* allow herself to be hurt again. Unfortunately, as the wall grew, her faith was quickly diminishing. She no longer thought there was any hope for her marriage. The depression and sadness were affecting her health. The only thing she could control was the amount of food she ate and didn't eat. Even when she wanted to eat, she was unable to do so. In some twisted way, she supposed it might be a cry for help. The thinner she became, the more she longed for someone to ask her, "Is everything okay?" Eden wanted someone to help her, notice her, and tell her she wasn't wrong for feeling angry and confused! She wanted validation that her eating disorder was just a manifestation of her inner pain. Who was going to believe her? What proof did she have of the pain she was going through? Heath had everyone fooled! Her family, friends, and the people at church thought he was the sweetest, most humble, gentle man in the world! They would never see him as a man who was capable of mistreating a woman or saying harsh, demeaning things behind closed doors.

April 5, 1995
Dear Diary,

Well, things got pretty bad with us. So I wrote him a four-page letter telling him how I felt. It worked! It was like a second honeymoon. Things have been so much better. Thank you, Lord, again!

May 12, 1995
Dear Diary,

Well, Heath came home today (8:00) after telling me to plan an evening with my friend, and he absolutely (—) me out! All because I didn't have dinner for him. I thought he'd eat out or something. I mean he nailed me! Let me tell you, if my son was not here, neither would I be! He sucks all my joy out! Signed, Extremely Sad!

Eden did not know how to act anymore. Every day she walked on eggshells, unsure of what to say or not to say, what to do or not to do. She began to pray more consistently for God to help their marriage and for Heath to stop talking to her so harshly. She didn't believe in divorce, and she never wanted her children to go through it. Her parents had a wonderful marriage. Fighting, or using ugly words, was never an issue for them. She constantly asked herself, "How and why is it happening to me?" Based on her understanding of the Bible, she didn't have any biblical grounds for divorce. As a Christian who wanted to please God, what was she supposed to do? She felt trapped in her marriage, and she didn't know how much longer she could endure the daily turmoil. She was so tired of feeling like she wasn't worthy to breathe the same air Heath breathed. She knew it was a very unhealthy environment for James as well. She knew God had to deliver her from the situation, or she was going to crash and burn. She also understood God would not help those who were unwilling to help themselves; she had to be responsible for her own actions. Once again, she tried to suck it up and prayed that Heath would eventually become aware of how he was treating her and be willing to change.

May 16, 1995
Dear Diary,

Sunday was Mother's Day. My husband didn't buy me a card from himself or my son. I told him how sad and disappointed I felt. I never thought he'd be this way. Oh well.

September 13, 1995
Dear Diary,

Did you know that he didn't get me anything for my birthday! Not a card from himself or even James. Can you believe this guy! Who did I marry?

Eden was not sure why Heath never bought her a card or gave her gifts on special occasions. When she asked him about it, he never could give her an answer. She was never someone who expected an expensive gift, but she did think it was important to be appreciated and recognized on special days, no matter who you were. Not once during their marriage had Heath given her a card! She often thought of her childhood. Her dad always gave her mom gifts and cards. Her mother did the same in return. Maybe she was expecting too much from Heath, but she really didn't think so. It just never made sense, and it was hurtful every time.

James was two years old, and her days were becoming very busy. Eden was still singing frequently at church and often felt overwhelmed as she tried to care for an active toddler and keep up with other responsibilities. Ironically, Heath was also singing for many events; therefore, it was common for them to be involved with some outside activity almost every night of the week. They started travelling out of the state singing in revivals, leading worship, and performing small concerts. Eden loved to sing but became weary with all the events because they required hours of preparation and memorization. She even grew tired of being around people all the time. Although she was honored to be a part of these activities, she needed rest. Her heart was too heavy, and her voice was tired. "Lord, please give me rest," she prayed.

October 13, 1995
Dear Diary,

Guess what? I'm pregnant! I decorated the door for Heath, and he came through the wrong door. I made him come through the decorated door. I guess he's excited. He still hasn't called his parents. He's feeling doubtful I suppose. Oh well. He comes home his usual self. I hate it! I hate it! I hate it! He made me cry. I'm so numb to him it's not even funny. I want to celebrate this pregnancy, but I am leaving it up to him. Which will never, ever happen! Signed, Confused! My due date is June 1996.

Her excitement turned into fear when she woke up the next morning with an extreme headache, fever, and vomiting. She took medication throughout the day, but the headache only got worse. She went to the doctor, and they dismissed her symptoms as severe pregnancy sickness. Later that week, she was unable to move her neck, and the constant headache, along with the vomiting, became so severe she decided to go to the emergency room. When she arrived, they promptly recommended a CT scan and spinal tap. These tests revealed that she was positive for bacterial meningitis. Unknown to her, there were several cases of viral and bacterial meningitis in the city where she lived. The pain was indescribable. She understood pregnancy sickness and had her share, but the addition of this illness made her days and nights unbearable. She was going to be down for at least six weeks, maybe more. When she asked God to give her "rest," severe sickness was not exactly what she had in mind!

October 22, 1995
Dear Diary,

Monday I woke up with a bad headache, which got worse and worse. Tuesday I went to the doctor, and I almost passed out it hurt so badly. Wednesday I went back to the doctor, and they gave me a shot, which only put me to sleep. Thursday evening it hurt so bad I went to the emergency room! They tested me, and I had viral meningitis! Bacterial can be deadly! It's been the most pain I've ever been through! I really missed and needed my family this week. Heath, however, has been perfect in every way! Thank you, Lord, for your healing power!

The people from their church were absolutely wonderful! They had so many meals prepared for them they had to share it with their friends. Of course, Eden was so sick she couldn't eat anything they brought to her. Nonetheless, she was blessed beyond measure and was so thankful for the generous acts of kindness from her fellow church members! She had never been so sick in her life. She was unable to leave the house for several weeks. Her sweet little James would climb onto the countertop and make his own lunch. He had to do many things for himself, because she was too sick to stand upright. He watched videos all day to keep himself entertained, but Eden felt guilty about it. She had no family living close by, so there was no one to help her. She really needed help with James, but there was no one to ask. Heath had been very helpful at the beginning of her illness, but as time progressed and her sickness lingered, he became very frustrated with her and resented having to help her. That, of course, was very hurtful to her. After his accident, all she did was take care of him while also caring for a new baby. She knew how difficult it was to do everything for someone who was unable to function independently. Now she needed his help, and she didn't have it. *Through sickness and in health*, she thought as she recalled their wedding vows to each other, but somehow Heath must have forgotten.

November 5, 1995
Dear Diary,

I have been so sick with this pregnancy. The doctor gave me suppositories to stop throwing up. They're working. I've been able to get up now. Heath has just complained. He's been his old butt again. He can be so hurtful! I really feel miserable. I know if I didn't have kids, I would have left. I hate the way he treats me and talks to me. He never does anything for me or with me. Oh well, where do you go when you know you've made a huge mistake?

Despite Eden's illness, the pregnancy progressed very well, and they discovered they were having another boy. Her unborn baby was growing and seemed to be very healthy. It took about three months for the meningitis to completely dissipate, allowing her to return to normal activities. She was starting to feel much better and felt that life was manageable again. James was going to be three years old in April, and they had chosen a name for the new baby due in June. His name would be Connor Davidson. James was so excited about becoming a big brother, and Eden knew he was going to be a great help to her. Her greatest concern, of course, was her marriage and whether it was going to survive. Was she wrong for bringing another life into this dysfunctional home? She already knew the answer, but Eden trusted the Lord to make it right.

June 21, 1996
Dear Diary,

Well, I am home from the hospital with Connor! He was born on the nineteenth at 9:37 a.m. Heath was great! He has dark hair like his dad and brother. He's perfect. James does very well with him! Good night, finally done!

I was asked to sing two weeks after delivery for the July Fourth program and a wedding. I am not sure why I held to those obligations, but I did. That started the trickling effect of my heavy schedule once again. My husband's work kept him away all the time. He was never home anymore. The times he did come home, we had singing obligations. There needed to be a healthier balance so he could see the boys more and maybe we could have some quality time together, if ever possible.

September 27, 1996
Dear Diary,

He works all the time! Never here for breakfast, and lately dinner and nights. We're never together, but he makes me so mad I don't want to be with him. He's a hard worker, but I have no respect for him! I don't know what to do! I do not respect him spiritually, romantically, or as a disciplinarian. What do I do? Oh well.

October 5, 1996
Dear Diary,

He works all the time and sleeps in the guest room. He cares about nothing except work.

November 6, 1996
Dear Diary,

He has spent no time with me. My life is ... scary.

Many unpleasant thoughts began to circulate through Eden's head. Was there someone else? Was he not attracted to her? Eden had always tried to keep herself in shape, and she always tried to look pretty for him. She wanted him to desire her and no one else. Did he just not love her, or even like her? As she reflected back over their marriage, she never had actually believed that Heath truly loved her. She had voiced her concerns to him on several occasions and even wrote him a four-page letter, trying to express her feelings to him. She didn't know what else it was going to take for him to understand how distraught she was with their relationship. She was astonished, however, that despite their personal troubles, God continued to use them in the music ministry. In fact, they had several people approach them concerning the possibility of going into the ministry full-time. Eden knew Heath had a desire to be working full-time in the ministry, but due to their circumstances, she was unsure of how she felt about it. She began to think that maybe their struggles were possibly stemming from not being in God's will. After all, if you are living in the "center of God's Will," aren't things supposed to run smoothly? At least, that's what she had always believed. Maybe Heath was unhappy because he was not serving where God wanted him, and they just needed to pray and seek a completely different direction for their lives. All she knew was that something needed to change before everything became worse.

January 22, 1997
Dear Diary,

Today was okay till about ten minutes ago. I have felt so cold toward Heath for years. He starts working on it and expects me to just jump in and be okay. It doesn't work that way. Yesterday was bad! I went to the bathroom to remove my makeup, and he makes his usual comment about how long I stay in there. I got angry and threw my wet rag on the floor. He picked it up and threw it at my face (three feet away). It really hurt and still stings! He was holding Connor! Now it is 10:00 p.m. Are we talking about it? Praying about it? No. I want out! How? I want out for the boys' sake!

Once again, as Eden always did, she tried to overlook her own pain, encouraging herself by praying and reading scripture. She also wanted God to provide direction concerning whether they should be serving full-time in ministry. She read these words in 2 Corinthians 6:2–10: "For He says: 'In an acceptable time I have heard you, and in the day of salvation I have helped you.' Behold, now is the accepted time; behold, now is the day of salvation. We give no offense in anything that our ministry may not be blamed. But in all things we commend ourselves as ministers of God: in much patience, in tribulations, in needs, in distresses, in stripes, in imprisonments, in tumults, in labors, in sleeplessness, in fasting; by purity, by knowledge, by longsuffering, by kindness, by the Holy Spirit, by sincere love, by the word of truth, by the power of God, by the armor of righteousness on the right hand and on the left, by honor and dishonor, by evil report and good report; as deceivers and yet true; as unknown, and yet well known; as dying, and behold we live, as chastened, and yet not killed; as sorrowful, yet always rejoicing; as poor, yet making many rich; as having nothing, and yet possessing all things."

March 17, 1997
Dear Diary,

Well, it has finally happened! We are going to go into the music ministry! A couple of weeks ago, our pastor was on a cruise with my brother. The pastor asked my brother if Heath had ever considered going into the music ministry and said that he should pray about it. Not to mention all the other people (including good friends that are in the ministry) who are thinking the same thing! I never thought we had what it takes (especially with all our problems)! But Friday I took Heath to the airport. He goes to A2, and guess who was there—our pastor! So they were able to talk more! We both knew that was God! So we're making steps toward schooling and ministry! Thank you, God!

The thought of moving and starting over again, now with two children, was unnerving for Eden. On the other hand, she became convinced that their stress and ongoing problems were the result of not being in God's will. She was very nervous, but she had to trust the Lord that Heath had truly been called by God to serve in the ministry. Heath needed to go back to school so that he could be fully prepared as he began this new venture. He applied to several schools and narrowed it down to a school in the Southwest. Their next step was to sell their house and make plans to move—again. Eden knew if God wanted them to go, He would take care of all the details.

April 6, 1997
Dear Diary,

Wow, so much has happened! This morning, we gave our testimony for an SS class! They took a love offering fifty-one dollars! That covered our school application fee! Plus sixteen more! Then a couple came to our house this evening. They want it! Wow! God is in this! I am getting excited. I can't stand it! Thank You, Jesus! I am so happy.

Eden felt that God had confirmed their decision. Their home was sold within one week of their decision to move, and many church friends helped them financially. Moving is always stressful but particularly difficult when you have to move quickly. Their house was sold, and they needed to find new living arrangements. It was all happening so quickly! Eden's parents were living in the North at the time, so she and Heath made plans to live with them during the summer months until school started in the fall. It was going to be an emotional move for Eden. She did not want to leave her close friends and church family again, nor did she want her boys to go through the changes she constantly endured as a child. She wanted stability for her boys. She was happy living in this town, but she was willing to move if this would help Heath and their marriage. She knew they would have many financial challenges due to moving expenses, tuition, and possible months of unemployment. They began praying for their future living arrangements and their financial and employment needs. Right now, they needed $860 to rent a moving truck and pay the first semester of tuition. They were trusting God that everything would fall into place. They were moving completely on faith.

May 30, 1997
Dear Diary,

Well, things are going fine. No real problems. I have a very sore throat and have to sing four times this weekend. Anyway, our pastor gave us $2,000 for school! We found out we were accepted too! Mom comes Wednesday. Then we pack! I've got real weird feelings about everything! I will miss my friends so very much!

June 25, 1997
Dear Diary,

A lot has happened! We closed on our house June 11 and moved out the twelfth. We left town Friday the thirteenth and arrived on Sunday. We sang last Sunday evening and received $861 from friends in a jar. It paid for our moving expenses! When we left town, we stopped by to visit my grandparents and then travelled on to my parents' house. We are tired! I miss everyone already! I'm getting really scared. I sure hope my husband doesn't back out. I'm afraid of what I will do.

Eden was trying to cope with a myriad of emotions—excitement, uncertainty, anxiety, gratitude, joy, and fear. She couldn't describe exactly how she was feeling. She wanted to believe they were going in the right direction, but she didn't trust her unstable marriage. She could see that God was fighting for them through affirmation of their attempt to serve Him and also by what He was doing in their lives. However, Heath's personal drive to serve in the ministry and earn his music degree superseded his desire to improve their marriage. She knew he did not understand the depth of restoration she needed. It was essential for him to change the way he was talking to her, and they needed to spend time with each other. There needed to be rekindling of a fire that had died long ago. Eden knew that it was important for her to honor and respect her husband. She also knew that he was to love her as Christ loved the church, but she absolutely had no respect for him, and his cruel words to her prevented her from wanting to honor him in any way. Her heart was so divided! One thing was certain. If she and Heath were going to serve in the church as leaders, things were going to have to change.

Chapter 6

Got Ministry?

There were three words that described where Eden and Heath were now living: hot, hot, and hotter! She had forgotten how blazing the sun could be in the desert. Eden wasn't sure where the Lord would send them after Heath graduated, but she was praying for a lot of trees and easy access to a large body of water. They had been in their new home only a few weeks, and she already had a list of prayer requests for their next move after graduation. She had to admit, a part of her restlessness was related to how she had grown up. Even though she disliked moving so often, it was hard not to look ahead and think about what might be next for her in the near future. One might think she lived in a constant state of discontentment; maybe she was. Eden had heard the statement, "The grass isn't greener on the other side; it is green where you water it." Very true, but she always wanted to know what was happening on the "other side" and make sure she wasn't missing out on another opportunity. One thing was certain; others may have referred to her as someone who was restless, unsettled, discontented, unhappy, or just bored, but for Eden, sometimes the word "change" was welcoming. Eden began to see how God had molded her through multiple changes in her life, and now, entering the ministry, she was hoping for a different change—her marriage.

August 5, 1997
Dear Diary,

Well, we left my parents' house on the first of August, Friday. We are trying to find work and a place to live. It is very frustrating and depressing! I might add ... scary too! The people are very friendly and helpful. James is four years old, and Connor is finally walking! He is thirteen months old.

Eden's faith began to grow as she saw answers to the smallest details of her prayers. Prior to moving, she had prayed for a place to live and for the boys to have a good place for to play. She took the time to make a prayer list, requesting some of their needs, and she even made a list of wants, primarily just for fun. She wasn't sure why she had dreamed of these specific items, but she told the Lord how nice it would be to have wooden floors, a fireplace, and French doors in an old house. She was firmly believing in Matthew 7:7, "Ask and you shall receive. Ye have not, because you ask not."

August 29, 1997
Dear Diary,

Well, a lot has happened! My husband found a job! He will be driving again. We also found a house on Wednesday. It's a cute old home with green awnings on all windows. It has 1,320 square feet, two bedrooms, a dining room, large bathroom, huge backyard, and (private) one-car garage. It has French doors! Wooden floors! Fireplace! We have wonderful neighbors. One neighbor even let me borrow her lawnmower to mow. We are still looking for a church home. My son is longing for a friend and to be in school. I also have the opportunity to be an aerobics instructor at the recreational center and become certified. We have met a lot of people and a nice couple. That's all for now. *I'll be twenty-nine years old next week! I think he's forgotten ...

Eden was absolutely thrilled that God had provided so many of the smallest details she had asked for. Her smallest prayer requests had been answered. This caused her to wonder if she had possibly missed out on many joys in life because she didn't ask, or maybe she was just not paying attention to what He was doing for her. She truly believed He knew what was best for her, and she needed to trust Him and just ask! After all, there were only three answers He could give—yes, no, and wait. What did she have to lose? God had been gracious to her and gave her what she asked for, but she soon found out that sometimes what we think we want isn't always what we need.

Eden loved her little old house, but it certainly wasn't perfect. The floor in the house slanted, causing the furniture to slide and not be stable. There was no central heat, and there was a lot of mold around the floorboards where the boys slept. But the house had wooden floors and a beautiful fireplace with French doors that had real crystal doorknobs, leading into the dining room. This was exactly what she had prayed for! She was very proud of their home, and she loved working in the yard. Unfortunately, they could not afford lawn equipment. The front was framed by large, grassy areas on the side, opening into the large, fenced-in backyard. Her neighbor was kind enough to lend Eden her lawnmower, but Eden wanted the lawn edged. She decided to take a pair of household scissors and cut the entire edge of the yard by hand! The yard was extremely manicured and looked beautiful, and she was very proud herself. However, the next day, the painful blisters on her fingers caused her to think twice about ever using scissors for landscaping again.

She also discovered that the neighborhood wasn't very safe. Many nights, Eden would lie awake listening to gunshots. The young people across the street were members of a gang. They were friendly to Eden and Heath, but their lifestyle was very unnerving, to say the least. Heath worked a full-time job at night and went to school during the day. She was at home alone with the boys most of the day and every night. One night, she was awakened by a helicopter that seemed to be circling their neighborhood. As she lay in her bed motionless, she nervously watched as the helicopter's spotlight flash through her window every few minutes. It was evident they were in search of someone on foot. Her bedroom was located in the back of the house where it was very dark, and her two sweet little boys were sound asleep in the front room of the house. Eden was frightened, so she began to pray. She gathered up enough nerve to turn on a light, and she picked up her Bible. When she opened it, the pages fell open to Proverbs 3:24, "When you lie down, you will not be afraid; yes, you will lie down and your sleep will be sweet." Eden thanked the Lord for His peace and His assurance. She closed her eyes and finally fell asleep.

She and Heath were struggling financially. His work hours had been cut back, and she was just working part-time as an aerobics instructor. The house payment was an overwhelming burden, particularly when you added it to the other debts they had accumulated. Eden began taking the boys to a local church every Tuesday for free food. They stood in line for two hours waiting for food the grocery store discarded, because of the past expiration dates. On Thursdays, Eden went to the school, along with other students, and stood in their line for free food. It was a blessing to have the food, but it was a difficult thing to do. She always checked the food carefully to make sure it was not spoiled. Each box of food would only last a couple of days, and she would have to go back and stand in the long food lines again. Once again, stress became almost unbearable. She had no idea how long she could keep living like this, and she didn't think their marriage could withstand this degree of difficulty. She was fine without food, but it was very difficult not having anything for her boys; it was not fair for them. Eden had many recipes for rice and peanut butter, but to grow strong, her boys needed some protein and vegetables. She questioned whether Heath's education was worth giving up their health and safety.

Regardless of the circumstances, Heath remained the same. Eden thought this call to ministry would change the way he saw her, spoke to her, and treated her. Their lives were in constant turmoil. "Does he blame me?" she wondered. She couldn't help notice that he didn't treat anyone else like he treated her. No one else had seen or heard the side of him that she knew! "So what is it about me, compared to others, that upsets him so much?" she constantly asked herself.

January 14, 1998
Dear Diary,

Life has been so hard lately! Heath hasn't worked in weeks, and he is taking it out on everyone, mainly me. He has made me feel worthless, taking everything I say wrong and to the extreme! I hate him! I'm so sick of his inconsistency! I wish so much I could get out of this relationship! I gave it all to the Lord and felt great till Monday when he made a very demeaning statement. Tuesday he did it again! I was already feeling lonely, depressed, with nothing to offer ... I did not get the front desk job at the school. I thought for sure I would get it. I was very embarrassed and disappointed when I didn't even get a call telling me why! Oh well, I am going for my step certification in February. He has never been there for me; it's all him! All him! He won't talk to me or be with me at all! He won't apologize! So what do I do? What do I do? Good night.

Eden couldn't help but observe other couples and wonder if they were truly as happy as they appeared to be. She had never been jealous or envious of material things, but she found herself growing very envious of her friends' happy marriages and families. She knew it was common for couples to have financial difficulties, maybe because her parents struggled financially when she was a child. But she also knew how it affected people. She knew their finances were creating major issues in their marriage, but she also knew that money, or lack of, was definitely not the root of their problem. Their struggles were much deeper than anything related to finances. They were coexisting in a dysfunctional, angry relationship, and she wished she could fully understand the reasons behind the chaos. Whatever the source, she wanted to escape the bondage she was living in.

The time came that she and Heath had reached the bottom of the barrel. They had run out of money, food, and gas—everything. They had been to the pawnshop on several occasions to sell items for extra money. They had decided not to sell their wedding rings, unless there was no other option, but it appeared that this was inevitable. On one occasion, James went to the refrigerator to get something to eat, but he opened it to find nothing inside except a bottle of ketchup. James turned to her and smiled. "Look, Mommy, just ketchup!" Eden began to cry. What were they going to do? In desperation, she began to pray, and she begged the Lord for help. "Lord, if you called us out here, you have to provide! Please!" About that time, Heath walked through the door with bags of groceries. His wedding band was missing.

January 16, 1998
Dear Diary,

Wow! Wow! You won't believe what has happened! Yesterday, Heath was so upset he left for a few hours. He came back with groceries! He had sold his wedding ring for $250! This morning we were so upset with life and each other! He was just about to drop out a semester to work *and catch up! We had to pay $260 the fifth of every month for four months to pay for tuition. We were not going to have it. Especially since he had not been able to work. Well, last night I just so happened to share our situation with our friends. We had all been trying for the past six months to get support from Christian Support Ministries located in Florida. We never could get through. Our friends were contacted yesterday to offer money for school tuition. Our friends declined the scholarship and told them about my husband, our circumstances, and how he sold his ring. This morning, a man called my husband from the Support Ministries team and spoke with him for an hour about his purpose and ministry. He has $800 he is going to send us for tuition! And out of his own pocket, he called the jewelry store and bought back the wedding ring for $200 more than we were given for it. Wow, how the Lord blessed us! We just can't believe it! Now my husband's work called, which is a blessing! Thank you, Lord, oh thank you!*

One month later, the man that bought Heath's ring back from the pawnshop also paid his tuition in full for a total of $1,015.13! Eden and Heath never met the man, and they never heard from him again! He was an angel from God, an unbelievable miracle, and they would never forget what God had done for them. Eden questioned why God would have them go to the extreme of selling Heath's wedding ring, despite their marital difficulties. But she realized that they would have never experienced such an awesome miracle if they had not been in such an extreme situation. Their difficult circumstances compelled them to make hard decisions, place their trust in God, and learn how to be faithful in all things, through all things, and with all things. Philippians 4:19 says, "And my God will meet all your needs according to the riches of His glory in Christ Jesus." She was amazed at God's work in their lives, in spite of their broken marriage.

February 27, 1998
Dear Diary,

James asked Jesus to come into his heart! He'll be five years old in April. God will let him know if it wasn't genuine. But I believe it was! He knows! I'm so, so, so excited! God is so good! Thank you, Lord, so very much!

The house payment was simply too much for them to pay on such a tight budget, so they moved into a townhome located on the school campus. It was an answer to prayer. They were able to save on gas and rent, and Eden was closer to the recreation center where she was employed. This allowed her to walk to work with the boys. She was teaching more aerobic classes and started working part-time as a preschool teacher in the mornings so her boys could attend free of charge. Heath's workload increased, and school, of course, was full-time. Eden loved living on campus, and she made new friends. The school required their townhomes to be occupied by couples with children, so there were plenty of children for the boys to play with. Eden and Heath became very close friends with the other parents, sharing Thanksgiving dinners, birthdays, and other holidays together. Eden and the boys embraced their new friendships. She was hungry for relationships, especially since she was home alone so much. Eden and the other mothers in the neighborhood had a common bond, because they all had children because their husbands attended school and worked full-time. Eden often wondered if the other women had a secret life behind closed doors. Surely they all struggled with something. Slowly but surely, she developed another hidden struggle—she was envious of her friends' marriages.

March 29, 1998
Dear Diary,

I'm so sick of Heath! It would be perfect without him! He always complains to me about everything! Never uplifting me or making me smile. I am so scared! I don't care anymore. He's not a man of his word at all! He never takes time to do anything with me or all of us. I don't know how much more I can take or how much more God will take of all this.

Their seventh-year anniversary had come and gone, and once again they did nothing for each other. Eden had given up; she was numb toward her husband. She was scared and nervous about their future ministry and if it was going to work. Eden began to daydream of what her life could have been like "if" ... That was an unhealthy state of mind. Evil seeds of destruction were starting to grow within Eden's soul. The seeds of desirous thinking—the "I wonder if ...," the "if I had only ...," and the "I wish I had ..."

October 2, 1998
Dear Diary,

Well, I've never been so busy. I'm keeping a little girl ten hours a day, teaching three aerobic classes, teaching three days at Mother's Day Out, plus church and homeschooling. I can't wait to go home and see my parents December 4! We're out of here! I told (my husband) I wasn't coming back till he was better. Man, we can't say anything without fighting. I hate our marriage. I've said that for six years now. I constantly think of where I could be in life and possibly who it could be with. I'm tired of living and not enjoying life, and my kids don't either. It has been detrimental to us. We will never be right!

Eden was determined to keep her mind on the Lord and stay focused on what He had called them to do. God had delivered them through too many circumstances and trials to question Him or His calling in their lives. Again, she turned to scripture, Philippians 3:12–14, "Not That I have already attained, or am already perfected; but I press on, that I may lay hold of that for which Christ Jesus has also laid hold of me. Brethren, I do count myself to have apprehended; but one thing I do, forgetting those things which are behind and reaching forward to those things which are ahead, I press toward the goal for the prize of the upward call of God in Christ Jesus."

Heath had been in school for two years when he received a phone call from a church several states away, wanting to interview him for a staff position. Heath had two years remaining in school to earn his degree, so he did not want to pursue the opportunity. However, the church was very persistent, so Heath agreed to visit with them and move forward with the interview.

March 28, 1999
Dear Diary,

To make a long story short, we visited a church last weekend. It's perfect! The pastor and all of us hit it off big time! They will pay for Heath to finish school and pay a salary. We will have a home, my boys a nice school, and I won't have to work. I can stay home with the boys! The church, people, staff, situation is perfect! We accepted and will be going out there in May and moving in June! God is so good! I love you, Jesus!

Eden could not believe it—it was happening again! Another move, but this time it was a completely different situation than ever before. They were going to be on staff at a small church, and she was so excited! The pastor had specifically asked Eden to help with the youth because of her experience in previous churches. He wanted her to implement some ideas and programs that would help the youth group grow. Heath had never held a staff position before, so she was more than willing to get involved and support his ministry by helping with the youth.

Heath finished the semester in school, and they moved to the small, quaint southern town to start their new ministry. Heath was hoping to continue school while he served in this new position. They moved into a beautiful home off a gravel road that was nestled deep in trees on the river, just what Eden had prayed for when she had first moved to the desert. God's direct involvement in her life never ceased to amaze her! Their new home had three bedrooms, a study, a living room, dining room, family room, a large kitchen, and laundry room. It was perfect! When Eden and Heath arrived, the church members had put welcoming signs in the yard and filled the cabinets and pantry with food. The biggest blessing was when James went through the cabinets, smiled, and said, "Look, Mommy! Food! Look how God blessed us!" James learned at an early age how to depend on the Lord for daily necessities. Eden was blessed to hear her son spontaneously give thanks to the Lord when he recognized God's provision.

She enrolled James in school, and he started the first grade. She had previously been homeschooling, so James was enjoying public school. Eden was also enjoying not having to homeschool so that she could spend more time with Connor. She began actively pursuing new avenues of outreach in the youth department and at church. After speaking with many of the women and youth in the church, she became involved in several requested programs and stepped in to fill some needed positions. Eden started a weekly aerobics program, a Wednesday night youth choir, and Tuesday night youth visitation program. She began teaching youth Sunday school and the youth group on Wednesday night. Eden also planned the youth banquets for holidays and graduation and even planned a mission trip to Midwest, which youth could earn through participating in a discipleship training program. She exhausted herself and her resources, but she loved every minute of it, and the youth were flourishing. The young people would come over to their house and play games; sometimes they skipped school just to hang out with her. James and Connor absolutely loved it when the youths spent time with them.

August 20, 1999
Dear Diary,

He has been so mean to me. I stopped loving him a long time ago. He just yelled at me for not wanting to go hear some group sing, totally insulting me. Now he is playing with boys like it is no big deal. I've lost every good thing I used to feel about him. I've stopped eating as of now. He will never understand how much he has and is hurting me!

As Eden walked through the local mall, she glanced in the display window of the Christian bookstore. The T-shirt read, "Got ministry?" She just stood there. *I just don't know anymore. I hope so,* she thought to herself. How could she describe this hidden turmoil that went on behind the scenes? How much longer could she hide it? Who could she talk to, or should she talk to anyone at all? Everyone seemed to love and respect her husband. They would never believe that he talked down to her, called her names, or yelled at her. Eden's walls were caving in around her. Every time they moved, her house and location would change, but for Eden, all of the houses had walls that felt like bars, as if it were a jail. She could see through to the other side, but she couldn't leave. She wanted out of a marriage and away from a man that had lost her love and respect. He had not touched her with his fist, but his mouth had torn Eden's heart out of her chest and thrown it away. Now that they were in the ministry, she was scared of the consequences of leaving Heath without a biblical cause to do so. Then suddenly, Eden's life turned upside down one more time.

March 9, 2000
Dear Diary,

Well, all (—) has broken loose around here. I just so happen to voice my opinion in the women's accountability group. It was only in reference to not memorizing scripture out of King James only! And not sharing our darkest secrets! God forgave me for things I did this past week! I don't feel like I have to bring those things up in front of them, especially if He has forgiven me already! Why give Satan another door to bring it up in my face? The pastor's wife let her husband know. The pastor and his wife called Heath and me in for a meeting. Four and a half hours long—my kids in the hall! The pastor let me have it! Absolutely destroyed me! He uplifted my husband so much but crucified me! I can't go into details; just know my spirit is broken! I hate going to church. I won't sing, I can't, the way he views me! And his wife went off on me too! Bye.

Never had Eden been scolded or demeaned by another man or person outside of her home. She was heartbroken, embarrassed, and completely devastated. She thought she had ministered to the youth and church well and had accomplished what the pastor had asked of her. Instead, she was specifically told that she was intimidating to the other women in the church and that she never brought the right Bible to church, if she brought one at all. Of course she brought her Bible to church … she taught the youth every week! She was reprimanded for always being late for the morning service and informed that she needed to come early and leave late, to set a good example. As the grueling conversation continued, the pastor proceeded to designate where she was to serve and where she didn't need to serve. For more than four and a half hours, she endured vicious attacks on her appearance, her ministry at the church, and her "ungodly" habits … as seen through the eyes of the pastor and his wife. They called it "Godly counsel"; she called it "ungodly venting!" Eden finally broke down and began to cry during the meeting. Then, and only then, did the pastor start apologizing for his behavior. It was as if he wanted to see her crumble under his authoritative leadership. He wanted to see her weak and broken down, as though he was disciplining a child. Perhaps worst of all was the fact that Heath sat quietly and nonchalantly at the end of the table. He said nothing the whole time! What kind of husband allows another man to humiliate his wife repeatedly, until she breaks down? How could Heath sit quietly, accepting all the praise and compliments they bestowed on him while dismantling his wife's character? What was wrong with him? Eden felt exposed and naked; she was confused, wounded, and totally broken. There was no one to defend her, not even the man to whom she had pledged her love and her life. She desperately needed an advocate, but there was none. She left the room, gathered her boys, and went home ... or was she just going to a house?

Ultimately, the pastor extinguished Eden's fire for ministry and shattered her heart. All the time, effort, energy, and love she invested in the youth and the church programs, he disgraced. She began to ask the same questions she had always asked herself: What am I doing wrong? What about me did he not like? But she also wondered why he was watching her so closely! Outside of her home, she had never encountered anything of this magnitude. Eden was in need of seeking Godly counsel outside of her church because she was unsure about her role in their ministry. Was she that messed up? Did God really not want her to serve in ministry, or was this just a pipedream she had invented to fill a huge void? She was clearly fighting two internal battles; her home was not secure, and her first place of full-time service in ministry had been shattered like a bullet hitting glass. Her spirit was numb, and her view of men in leadership had become misconstrued.

She finally came to the realization that she was trying to meet certain standards in order to feel good about herself. She understood it was natural to want to please people and herself; unfortunately, believing this only distorted God's truth. The false concept that she must be approved by certain others to feel good about herself had caused so much fear of rejection and doubt that she eventually conformed her attitude and actions to the expectations of others. If her performance did not generate the response she expected, she felt empty and confused. Eden desperately needed the approval of others, and when it wasn't given, she felt worthless.

Colossians 2:8, NKJV says, "Beware lest anyone cheat you through philosophy and empty deceit, according to the tradition of men, according to the basic principles of the world, and not according to Christ." Eden read that Paul wants us to be free in Christ, so she needed to recognize what was really important in her service and ministry. Eden's love for God and people was honest and true, but her earthly qualifications needed to be met by the approval of others or she felt like a failure. Galatians 1:10 says, "For do I now persuade men, or God? Or do I seek to please men? For if I still please men, I would not be a bondservant of Christ."

Eden was dreading the first Sunday back after everything happened, but she was amazed she was able to walk all the way to the front and sit in the front row! She was the "staff wife" standing tall with a painted-on smile, sharing warm hugs and welcoming handshakes. But as the church service began and she stared at Heath as he sat with a smile on the platform, something happened inside her soul. The music began to play as the audience stood to sing, but when she tried to open her mouth, her lips would not move; not a sound left her lips. Eden took notice of the large flower arrangement displayed in front of the pulpit. *How appropriate*, Eden bitterly thought to herself. *Those beautiful flowers will wilt by the end of the week; maybe they should have chosen plastic flowers.* She held back her tears as she stared at the stage, looking at the two men who had belittled, demeaned, and degraded her character. After years of abuse and neglect, Eden had lost her song.

July 3, 2000
Dear Diary,

Well, it's already July. I've been having a real hard time coping with it here. The mentality and possessive, obsessive attitude is driving me to a nervous breakdown! So much so I enrolled in school full-time and will work part-time. There is a church that is in touch with us. Heath and I cannot get along! The pastor has totally destroyed what we thought we were rebuilding! Plus, we were supposed to go to the zoo tomorrow for the Fourth. Heath was supposed to plan it. Guess what. It is midnight and nothing. But Mother's Day ... he did nothing for me or from the boys! I can't believe I married this inconsiderate jerk! My birthday and anniversary are coming up. I expect nothing! In fact, today I was sick with a headache, and my son took care of me, not Heath! I do not love this man! I really don't! Help!

Heath began to realize that their ministry had been suppressed, and if they chose to stay, things would never be the same. Eden's heart was torn. While somewhat apathetic toward her husband, she knew he was happy, and she did not want to bear the guilt of being responsible for them leaving the church or for having to move again. Her thinking was surely distorted, because deep inside her heart, she knew she wasn't to blame. She also didn't want Heath to have any more resentment for her, since he so quickly blamed her for the previous decisions they made that resulted in poor outcomes. Nonetheless, the time had come to make another choice to move—where, when, and how? Uprooting her boys another time was going to be extremely disturbing for her, as memories of her childhood haunted her. Her boys loved their home, friends, and church, so it was likely going to be very difficult for them to understand why they had to leave.

Heath received many calls from a few other churches, but he

was particularly interested in one and wanted to follow up with an interview for full-time staff position. The church would only require leadership in one department; therefore, Eden could stay home with the boys and volunteer in the church if she wanted to. Heath decided to talk with the staff and visit the facility. Eden was still mourning the realization that her boys were about to be uprooted again. She had been very pleased with their current school and was quite anxious about them having to start over. If they did move to the location of this new church, she knew they had the largest homeschooler association in America and also a large private Christian school. She was encouraged to have the two options for their education, because for her, the public schools were not an option. Heath and Eden really didn't want to move, but with their current situation, they felt it was inevitable. With much reluctance, Heath prepared to resign from his church staff position.

Their last night was very sad. The church members and youth did not understand why Heath resigned. Heath and Eden had given their hearts, energy, time, and love to these people, and the church members did the same for them. They never revealed the painful truth or the real reason for their leaving. There were a few staff members who understood, because they too had experienced the fiery scolding from the pastor. Heath and Eden really loved the people, and it was so difficult to say good-bye. They felt like they were leaving a family, and their children were leaving close friends as well as another school and home.

As they drove down the interstate, Eden stared out the window. Her heart was heavy. She feared they had made a bad mistake. This was the first open door of opportunity they had to escape their situation, a chance to start over. She wanted to trust Heath and herself with their decision, but one glaring fact remained. She didn't love him anymore, and even worse—she didn't love herself. She kept visualizing the image of the T-shirt, "Got ministry?" she saw displayed in the window at the mall. That simple question suddenly became very complex. Honestly, she was too afraid to answer, because deep inside she knew she was not fit for His service. Years of pain and struggle had finally caused her heart to be cold and numb.

December 16, 2000
Dear Diary,

Too much time has gone by! You won't believe how much has changed. We are only seven miles from the beach! We have a house with a pool. Yes we accepted a call to a church. It's not wonderful, but we are free. We enjoy it here, but there are a lot of frustrations on Heath's behalf. We are not sure why we are here, but God knows.

The Lord blessed Heath and Eden with a beautiful new home and another church family. There were some other adjustments with moving they all had to make. Needless to say, southern hospitality would be an attribute greatly missed. James and Connor had always been taught to say, "Yes, ma'am," or, "No, ma'am," "Yes, sir," "No, sir." Both adults and kids would tease the boys for being so "polite," but James and Connor stayed true to how they were taught. Eden was a proud parent; needless to say, she raised her boys to be respectful no matter where they lived in the United States. Besides, she was never sure how long they would live anywhere, so she taught boys to be faithful to God, to love themselves and each other, and to be respectful to all people.

March 24, 2001
Dear Diary,

Wow, it has been way too long since I have written, and so much has happened. I am four months pregnant! Not sure how this happened! What a total shock this was. I have been homeschooling, but James is so lonely. We are enrolling him in school. My heart breaks for him. He will be eight in three weeks, and we will not have a party because he doesn't have any friends.

Eden was able to be a stay-at-home mom with Connor and James. She liked the freedom of choosing her schedule, and it allowed her to always be available for her boys. However, James was having a difficult time in his new school and also at church. James was such a polite young man, and he truly loved God and people, with a little regard for race or social status. Eden discovered that many of the kids at school and at church were unruly and inconsiderate. She worried about James when he was away at school, wondering if he had anyone to play with on the playground, or if he was eating lunch alone. Maybe it was her own childhood fears coming back to haunt her, but as a mother, she could not help but worry all the same. To complicate matters, Heath was also having a difficult time adjusting to his new staff position. It was just not the same, although the people and pastor seemed friendly and tried to make them feel welcome. Heath simply didn't feel the connections he had experienced in the previous church. Both Eden and Heath remained sad over the loss of precious relationships with people they loved but understood they needed to press on and fulfill what they believed God had called them to do.

August 22, 2001
Dear Diary,

Well, Monday was James's first day of school—third grade! He was in class with two girls he knew from church. He had a lonely lunch and recess but had a good day all in all. Tuesday was much better. He was picked by some boys to play soccer. I pray today is better. Last night was really bad! Heath said some extremely demeaning things to me and about me in front of the boys. Then he left for visitation. I am so tired and lonely. I am due in four weeks.

The insults and degrading remarks from Heath became worse. Eden assumed he was unhappy with her because they had to move again. Maybe Heath had been upset with her from the beginning of their marriage, because if it had not been for her, he would still be living in the Midwest where his family lived. Who knew? She didn't really think it was her fault, but she had conditioned herself to believe the lies—that she was to blame for anything that went wrong.

Eden was more concerned about the demeaning comments Heath was using in front of James and Connor. She was expecting another little boy in a few weeks, and there would be one more child for her to try to shelter and protect. The boys were old enough to understand what was being said, and she never wanted them to be exposed to angry conversations filled with unkind words. She wanted their home to be a haven for them, and she longed to set a good example for them. She wanted them to learn to be patient and loving, even in the midst of controversy or disagreements. Listening to their dad belittle their mother and call her names was contradictory, not only to how she was teaching them, but it was not exemplary of a Christian home with a God-centered marriage. Now she was bringing another little boy into the world, and he deserved Godly role models and a safe and loving home environment. To say the least, Eden was very worried.

Time quickly passed, and the baby was due in less than a week. James was in school when she and Connor were watching cartoons. Several cartoons later, Eden decided to turn the channel to watch the news. Standing in front of the television with the remote in her hand, she watched in horror and shock as an airplane flew into the New York Twin Towers. She would remember this as "the day our world stood still," better known as 9/11. Soon thereafter, Eden received a call from school informing her that she needed to come and get James. School was closing early, and there was total chaos! What a scary time to bring another child into the world! She felt that America would never be the same but found comfort in the knowledge that God had always been in control of everything, and she felt sure that He always would be.

Two weeks after America's devastation, Heath and Eden's little miracle arrived. Their beautiful son, Ronan Davidson, was born in September 2001. He was long, strong, and healthy. Eden never would have thought—three boys! What a blessing! All healthy, all long and lean, all with big feet, and all that didn't sleep! Yes, another boy that was up all night. Eden wasn't sure how she had given birth to children that did not sleep, but it was true. She tried every remedy that was supposed to help them sleep, but nothing seemed to work. Eden was so tired and sometimes lay in bed crying, "Lord, you closed the mouths of lions when Daniel was thrown into their den; why can You not close the mouth of this child?" Don't misunderstand. She loved her boys more than anything or anyone, but she was emotionally and physically exhausted. It never seemed to end.

Heath was staying at the church all day and most evenings. Eden was alone with the boys quite often. Ronan was starting to have breathing difficulties, and about every two or three weeks he would become very sick with respiratory problems. One evening in particular, Ronan began coughing, and it sounded serious. It was a rhythmic cough, one that Eden had never heard before, and she was unsure of what to do. James and Connor had been asleep for a couple of hours while she paced the floor, trying to console Ronan. Heath wasn't home, because he was meeting with someone who had visited the church that past Sunday. In desperation, Eden called him and told him what was going on. She begged him to come home, because she was frightened and didn't know what to do for Ronan. Heath refused to come home. He was "busy," and she could handle it on her own. Pacing the floor, her anger and frustration escalated as she continued to try to console her son. Should she call the ambulance? Go to the emergency room? Her boys were asleep, and she didn't know if this really was an emergency. She just felt that something was seriously wrong.

Frantically, Eden began to pray, and about ten minutes later, Ronan's coughing began to calm down, and he seemed to be crying normally. The next morning, she took him to the doctor, and he was diagnosed with asthma. She felt so guilty that she hadn't known what to do for him and didn't proactively seek help for him, but the greatest pain in her heart involved the realization that this precious baby's dad had chosen to put someone else first. It was just another dagger in her soul!

December 17, 2001
Dear Diary,

Well, Ronan is in his third month, and it has been horrible! He is the worst sleeper. I have been trying the schedule—nope! It doesn't work. My household has fallen apart—totally. Heath and I are over! We have been, but now it's really done. He's touched me one time since September, and he won't again for all I care or want! I hate marriage and the ministry. Well, it's no joy. Where did I mess up? I guess August 10, 1991. That's all I can explain. We've thrown in the towel and can't even talk about it. Where's God's mercy? I need encouragement, help ... love!

Heath's frustration where they were serving continued to build. Eden started to realize that their move was probably not the best choice for his ministry. Heath had the desire to finish his college degree, and serving full-time on staff at the church was not giving him the opportunity to return to school. Eden's brother was helping with the music program at the church and university up north. Heath had heard about the program and became very intrigued and wanted to enroll in the new program that was offered so he could continue his schooling. Eden refused to be involved in any more of their decisions so that she would not be blamed and held accountable for any more exhausting changes or mishaps in their lives.

After weeks of prayer, Heath made the decision to move and enroll in school once again. Honestly, the boys and Eden were excited to be closer to family and leave. The town they were currently leaving was a rude, rough place to live. They all had made friends, but it was not going to be as difficult to leave. They had not been there very long, and deep friendships had not been formed. In fact, Eden and the boys were ready to go. Heath put the house on the market for sale by owner, and the house was actually under contract within twenty-four hours! God chose to move very quickly and, as always, provided for their every need. Eden packed the house and the boys to move once again!

August 20, 2002
Dear Diary,

Wow! It's been forever since I've written anything! And so much has happened! Ronan is eleven months old, James is nine, and Connor is six. We left our home to move north where my family lives. We bought a brand-new home because we were able to sell our home. Within twenty-four hours! God totally blessed! Heath was offered a job at the university and working alongside the church with my brother and pastor! His schooling is paid for! I can't believe it! The boys start public school (which I feel much better about). They have met good friends at church already. It has been a blessing. I have lost a lot of weight, however, because of my marriage. I am also taking Zoloft. It is helping with my depression and anxiety. Oh! I led two women's retreats with five hundred ladies. I'm also flying to West Palm Beach in September to lead another one. I will speak in a classroom at the university in a few weeks. I am excited about ministry again! Thank you, Jesus! My son is sleeping! Finally!

Heath, Eden, and the boys finally arrived at their new home. It was surrounded by many trees, rolling hills, curvy roads, and best of all, Eden's family lived just a few miles away. Eden felt safe, and it was a comforting feeling to all of them! The degree Heath was pursuing would take two years. Maybe this would help their relationship. Perhaps Heath would now be more contented and things would change. One thing was certain; Eden was determined that Heath would finish school and hold that diploma in his hand!

She wasn't sure why the past four years of ministry had been so difficult and challenging. Maybe it was the result of their secret turmoil behind closed doors. Whatever the reason, the dreams and expectations she had for herself and their ministry ended quite differently. This was definitely not what she had thought it would be. She loved music, serving, and she loved people, but she found that things were very different when you were a paid staff member. Raised in the ministry, she was accustomed to traveling and attending different churches. But as a family, they would go and serve; then they would have to leave quickly, going on to the next church. She was never in a church long enough to see how the staff operated. She never knew how things functioned behind the scenes, and her parents never spoke negatively about the church. She had a great respect for them and admired them for always speaking positive words and being faithful to God, regardless of circumstances. As she pondered these things, she considered that maybe she wasn't really called to serve in the ministry, as she had previously thought. If Heath had truly been called by God to serve in this capacity, where did that leave her? How was she going to deal with these conflicting emotions about serving on staff again? Their track record wasn't good. If this was her calling, would she experience such mixed emotions? So, "Got ministry?" Maybe she just needed to find it again.

In 1 Corinthians 15:58, it says, "Therefore, my beloved brethren, be steadfast, immovable, always abounding in the work of the Lord, knowing that your toil is not in vain in the Lord."

Chapter 7

The Final Impact

Eden's heart was pounding with nervous excitement as she heard the beautiful music resonate throughout the auditorium. She smiled timidly, having almost forgotten how ghostly people in the audience appeared underneath the blinding stage lights. She took a deep breath and slowly lifted the microphone to her trembling lips. Her eyes quickly filled with tears as she began to hear her voice echo throughout the room. Suddenly, standing in the spotlight amid a blurred crowd of unknown faces, the Lord restored Eden's song! When the song ended, and as she walked off the stage, she was keenly aware that her heart was overflowing with joy and her spirit was full of hope. She felt a sense of freedom and that she now had been given the opportunity to leave the past few years behind her. After years of floundering through trials and errors in ministry, she was optimistic that she was on a new path, one that would lead to the restoration of her crumbling marriage.

She and Heath found their beautiful new home. With three bedrooms and a full finished basement, it was perfect for all of them, and the boys loved it too. They even bought the boys a dog, their first pet. Everything seemed to be picture perfect. Heath was excited about school and seemed to be more at peace with his new career. It was an added blessing that his tuition was free because he was a school employee. Heath and Eden's music ministry started to expand as they once again began singing for church services and at other events. Eden had also been invited to speak several times in various venues, which she thoroughly enjoyed. It was ironic, but she actually had more confidence when speaking than she did when singing. When she was speaking, she didn't have to worry about forgetting the words or messing up the notes. The boys were enjoying their new school and church family, making many new friends and fitting in quite nicely. Eden could rest peacefully during the day, knowing her boys were happy in their new schools. They lived in an area now that was quiet, safe, and conservative—a good place to raise children.

August 22, 2002
Dear Diary,

Yes! Last night, Wednesday, August 21, 2002, Connor asked Jesus into his heart! He has wanted to for a while but has been afraid! Heath was gone, but James and I prayed with him. He is so excited, so is my son! Thank you, Jesus.

Eden was beginning to believe they had finally reached a place in their marriage where they could start over and rebuild what had been torn down. Their marriage had been like a ship lost at sea, tossed around during a storm, with no direction and no hope of reaching the shore safely. The past few months, however, had been more peaceful. Eden was still dealing with the aftermath of previous hurts, but she was anticipating better days ahead for all of them.

James and Connor were in school, and Eden had been staying home with Ronan. Unexpectedly, she was offered a job as an aerobics coordinator for a local gym. This was a great job opportunity for her to advance as an aerobics instructor and develop her leadership skills. She was really excited and anxious to share the news with Heath. Unfortunately, when she told him about it, he was not excited for her at all! While he had always wanted her to work, he also wanted her to stay at home with the boys. Obviously, this scenario was not possible. This was only part-time, but she soon concluded that she would never be able to please him. She definitely wasn't sure of what to do about accepting this new offer.

After much consideration, she decided to accept the job and began working part-time while Ronan stayed in the nursery from nine until noon. She thought it was a good arrangement for both Ronan and herself. He could have some playtime with other children, and she could earn extra income. She noticed that she was experiencing a new sense of freedom. She only worked three hours in the morning and then taught an aerobics class a couple evenings a week. Eden had always exercised, mostly in the home, but now that she had access to the gym, she began working out there. Her family also had free access, which she felt was an added bonus. Heath didn't agree! As time passed, he became increasingly irritable and even spiteful. Their peaceful relationship was short-lived and was suddenly diminishing for no apparent reason. She didn't know if it was jealousy, a feeling of inadequacy, or just hatred toward her. She was convinced that he still did not like her, much less love her. She was beginning to realize that it was not going to matter where they lived, what jobs they had, what opportunities they were given. Heath was going to remain the same. Little by little, she began to isolate herself from him and deliberately looked for ways to avoid contact with him.

At the gym, Eden began a weightlifting program, and she was challenged to compete in a bodybuilding event. She had always thought it would be fun to compete, but she never knew how to train or what to do to prepare for a competition. Eden now had the opportunity to learn, and she took full advantage of it. She was still too skinny at the beginning of her program, so she was given a diet plan and exercise program that would help her gain some healthy fat as well as lean muscle. She had a difficult time eating and gaining weight because of her past issues with food. The program actually proved to be very healthy for her. Food now had a purpose! If Eden wanted to put on any muscle mass, she had to learn what to eat, how to eat, and when to eat. It helped her focus on taking care of herself again, allowing her to build confidence in eating in a healthy manner. For many years, the constant stress in her marriage and her low self-esteem had caused her not to eat properly. She literally became fearful of food. She knew she could control her eating and nothing else. It was like her own private rebellion against the world and herself. She didn't remember a time when she didn't feel actual pain in the depths of her being. It was like she was saying to her body, "You are hurting me, so I just won't eat. I will show you." Eden was suffering from anorexia, a silent disease that allowed her to control a small part of her daily life.

As she progressed in her weight-training program, she realized that physical strength bred mental strength. She grew more conscious of her own desires and needs. She didn't want to be called names anymore! She didn't want to hear Heath say, "What kind of woman does this?" when she had chosen to play with her boys instead of finishing the laundry. She didn't want to be criticized for not cleaning the house the way he wanted it cleaned. She didn't want to be told to pick up after herself like an adult. She didn't want to be told to pack her things and leave the house and "find another man," simply because her husband was in a bad mood. She didn't want to be called a lesbian in front of her boys, just for wanting to go see a girlfriend's new outfit before she went out on her first date. For certain, she never wanted to be told again to "go drown in a lake" for not having dinner ready! She did not want to be called a pig for eating too many popsicles, especially when she was already underweight. She was sick and tired of being sick and tired! From that moment on, she was determined that she would not allow

Heath, or any other man, to demean her again—at least without a fight! She had found her voice ... but it wasn't her singing voice!

January 2, 2004
Dear Diary,

Well, I won my first competition! First place (11/21/03)! It was awesome! I hadn't felt that confident and proud of myself ever! I am still training. I hope to win overall next competition and move up to pro! I love the training and the sport. Job is great, and I'm personal training now more than ever. Heath hasn't been supportive of my work at all. Even though financially I have to. Work is my life now; home sucks with Heath. It has for years. When we "talk," we fight; if we are together, it's for him only. He doesn't care what I like or need. We never laugh or go out. It's horrible. I guess it's been over for years. The only thing I hate is doing this to the boys! It's very hard to be happy around them or with them! I could never tell my family. They never would understand! And our so-called ministry would be over. So what is one to do? Live in misery because of everyone else? After the kids are in bed, I go upstairs, and he goes downstairs. Never talking, nothing! Sadly, I don't give a (—)! I just feel stuck! And have nowhere to go! My family would disown me, and Heath would take the boys. He doesn't even trust me! Even though I haven't done anything at any time with anyone! He doesn't love me or respect me! He blames everything on me, and I am the one who should sacrifice my time, life, and job! My job is the only thing keeping me happy and sane! I have no friends other than those at work! I don't have a lot of girlfriends, and it just so happens some of them are guys. I cannot help it if the girls don't want to hang with me. But I am not going to be lonely and depressed at home and lonely at work! I just don't get it! Christian friends suck! I've had no good friends here that are honest and trustworthy and not judgmental! I feel like a black sheep, and I haven't done anything! (Imagine that.)

Heath had absolutely no interest in Eden's career or the sport she had grown to love. However, he seemed to gloat over his new position and bragged about relationships with key leaders in the school and at church. He had a new sense of pride in himself that she had never seen before. It angered her to the point that she didn't want to be involved with church or his ministry anymore. His disposition at work and church were so contrary to the way he treated Eden at home. He was so respectful and kind to everyone else but extremely disrespectful and unkind to her. Eden wondered how he could be so different and entertained the thought that perhaps his inconsistent temperament would bleed over into his work, and others would realize the truth beneath his disguise. Eden no longer remained silent when Heath was rude to her; in fact, she quickly fought back. Maybe she was wrong to retaliate, because it really seemed to fuel the fire, but she wanted him to recognize what he was doing and stop! Heath became more spiteful, and their confrontations escalated as her bold responses to his ugly behavior revealed a new side of him. He became very controlling and domineering, frequently quoting scripture verses in an attempt to belittle her and make her feel inadequate as a Christian woman and mother. He was suspicious of every phone call and began stalking her. He called her friends, asking them questions about what she had been doing while at the gym and after work. Eden was not sure what she had done to unnerve him or make him feel so insecure, but she had a new situation on her hands, and it was very alarming.

April 14, 2004
Dear Diary,

James's eleventh birthday. I can't believe it! My other boys will be eight and three. Time is flying! Life again is very stressful. Heath and I are struggling. I've got no feeling for him. What a sad place to be, especially with three boys and living around family. Will life ever be fun? Will it ever provide relief? I still don't have any girlfriends at the church, not one. I have friends at work, but they are single—lucky! I know. I would give anything to start over, marry someone else, or better yet, not marry at all! I couldn't see. Where was my discernment? What was I thinking? Desperate, I suppose. It's hard for me to believe how much I once loved him. Bye.

The boys were old enough now to understand the conflict between Eden and Heath. It was beginning to take a tremendous toll on the entire family. The fighting was becoming more frequent and more violent. When Eden tried to avoid Heath, it only caused him to be more confrontational and agitated. She would often retreat to her safe place, the bathroom, to get away from him. But Heath would stand in the doorway so that she could not escape. His eyes were fiery, and his face was bright red as his mouth would vomit ugly, demeaning, thoughtless words. Eden would scream to the top of her voice, even hit him as hard as she could to get him to shut up. He would never stop! It was as if he took pleasure in seeing her react to his domination. He would just stare at her with wide, wild eyes and a crazy-like face, making accusations, continuously quoting scriptures, and undermining her as a mother and as a woman. She would literally have to fight her way out of the bathroom. If the boys were home, unfortunately, they too would try to pull him out of the doorway, yelling at him to stop and leave her alone.

September 23, 2004
Dear Diary,

Well, my birthday came and went. I got nothing from Heath. Not even a card. I am done with him. No more! I'm 110 percent done! I'd leave tomorrow, well, tonight actually, if I didn't have the boys. There would be no doubt

I'd be gone today! I know I've said it over and over before, but now it is over. We haven't been together (thank God) in over seven months. Haven't missed it—he grosses me out just touching me! Who'd of thought? So we go play this spiritual game, and yet we are in hell. So now what? The boys are feeling it too. So do we help them by staying or leaving each other? P.S. We did nothing for our thirteenth anniversary either.

Eden had reached a scary, unhealthy place in her life. It was dark and lonely, and her entire soul had become numb. She could not recall another time in her life that she had been so anesthetized to everything and everyone. Maybe it was a defense mechanism so she wouldn't get hurt anymore, but all of her feelings and emotions seemed to have shut down. Eden had lost all hope, and honestly, she just didn't care anymore. She was ready to end her marriage, but unfortunately, she didn't know how to get out. She was imprisoned in an unexplainable, horrific marriage, and not one other person on earth knew what she was going through!

Eden began spending more time away from home than usual. She could not stand the sight of her husband. Every time she was away from home, she realized she was sacrificing precious time with her boys. She felt caught in a terrible trap. She had discussed divorce with Heath, but he would not agree to it. He threatened her with the worst scenarios possible if she attempted to divorce him. He wanted full custody of the kids and for Eden to get out of the house, with no financial help from him. She tried to reason with him, explaining once again why she thought they needed a divorce. His critical words, demeaning comments, and their constant fighting were not a healthy environment for the boys. Didn't he understand that? She even told him she didn't think he loved her. She asked him, "What about me do you love?" The only answer he gave her, after all those years, "The way you look."

March 26, 2005
Dear Diary,

My heart and soul are crying. Heath was so out of line with me yesterday. I wish he'd just hit me—the pain would go away sooner! He is so jealous and suspicious about me, my work, and so on! Unbelievable! I can't get it right! I do everything wrong! I love what I do, but he hates it, and his words are devastating to me! He doesn't care anymore if it hurts. I'm lost, lonely, and so not knowing what to do or where to turn. I absolutely hate him! I'd give the world to be single again! He's even out of line with the boys; everything has to be perfect. I even have to take care of my son's bully at school. I had to talk with the teacher. (My husband) was there and didn't do a thing. He has never stood up for the boys or me. It's pathetic! I'm so exhausted all the time. I wish I could describe how I feel. Hopeless, lonely, desperate, trapped, hypocritical, tired, emotionless, empty, more lonely, ugly, fake, sick, and yes, lonely.

Another year had flown by, and nothing had changed; things had just become worse. Heath had pushed Eden so far over the edge she had fallen off the cliff. The devil's plan to destroy her was slowly developing. He knew the delicate, susceptible condition of her heart, and he knew exactly how to occupy space in her mind. With full understanding of her vulnerability, he stepped into her life through an open door, with an evil smile and a welcome mat under his filthy feet. There was no doubt he brought his small destructive army with him. They seemed to occupy her entire body; they traveled with her everywhere she went, and they influenced every decision she made. Little did she know that from this day forward she would never be the same again. Psalms 28:14 says, "Happy is the man who is always reverent, But he who hardens his heart will fall into calamity."

August 5, 2005
Dear Diary,

Again, it's been forever since I have written. I won first place in the Tall Class Figure competition. I had a lot of fun. (The pro MC) has been calling me about fitness modeling! Trying to hook me up with photographers. I'm trying to get some on my own, but it is not working well. Work is fine; sometimes I wish I didn't have to work. I still don't hang out with any girlfriends. In fact, no one at all. I have such a weird, unorganized, messed-up life. I am a horrible, confused wife and mom. I am miserably married and take it out on my kids. I hate this place now. I'm tired of being depressed and lonely—everywhere I go. The only good thing is that my boys like it here.

August 27, 2005
Dear Diary,

Things still suck—maybe even worse. I am so depressed I can't even get even get out of bed. I have no friends! None! I wish I were dead sometimes. I go to work, come home, and sit all day! That's it—every day! Heath hasn't even started school yet! Of course it's always my fault somehow, even though for fourteen years it's been about him! I wish we could split! I really do! I hate being married. I hate it!

Eden had stopped for gas on the way home from work one afternoon. She swiped her debit card and read the words "declined." She continued to swipe the card, knowing for certain there was enough money in their account to fill her tank. It was totally on empty, so she had no way of returning home. She called Heath. "Yes, I removed your name from our account. You no longer have access." She could not believe he had closed their joint account! He opened a new bank account in his name only, leaving her with nothing! "How can it take two people's signatures to open a joint account, and only one to close it?" Eden wondered with disgust. Her car payment and Visa card were in her name. How was she going to make those payments with only a part-time job? More important, and much more urgent, how was she going to get home without gas? Eden phoned a friend, who met her at the gas station and gave her money for gas and enough cash to pay for her next bill. What a true blessing, because she truly did not know what she was going to do. She had reached a point where she needed to tell her family that she wanted to divorce Heath and why.

The following week, she met with her family and told them the ugly truth of her life behind closed doors. She did her best to articulate the circumstances of her marriage and tried to describe what Heath's true behavior was really like. Their disbelief astonished her, and it only fueled her resentment and confusion. The secret she had kept for so many years now was out in the open. She had always dreaded the time when she would need to tell the truth, fearing that she might not be believed. Well, she was right. Her story seemed to make no sense to those she loved most. Immediately, she felt as though she had made a huge mistake. She felt defeated and alone. From her point of view, everything and everyone she trusted had failed her. Her husband had forsaken her; God had left her to fend for herself; and now her family wasn't providing any support for her. Eden wanted to die, but instead ... she completely self-destructed.

10/7/05
Dear Diary,

My family just left. I'm so depressed! It was a hard time for all of us. I told them everything about Heath and me. I told him I want papers. He said he would not sign. I asked him why. He never said, "Because I love you." It was every other answer. Because he doesn't and I don't love him! I'm tired of living what everyone else feels I should live. No one knows! That's it! I am ready to be happy and treated well! I want to do things, travel, go out to movies, laugh, or be touched! I have no life! I don't know how to get him out of my life!

October 16, 2005
Dear Diary,

Well, I still want a divorce; he said no. He continues to make my life (—)!

October 17, 2005
Dear Diary,

Heath doesn't get it! He, after twelve years, wants to get on medication, Prozac, go shopping, eat out, and so on with me! I don't want to! He is the last person on earth that I want to do anything with! He gets mad! I told him it's over; he doesn't get it. I'm at a loss! What is he thinking? He always wants to know what I am doing, where I am going, what I am doing, and calls me all day. Stop! Yuck! It is over!

Eden had reached the lowest point in her life. She felt as if she had nothing. Her parents and other family members moved several states away, and she had no one to turn to. She no longer attended church. To be honest, she had no desire to serve in the ministry in any capacity. She no longer wanted to sing, and the slightest thought of going to church sickened her. Little by little, she found herself fully rebelling against everything in which she had formerly trusted. There seemed to be no shred of hope in the depths of her soul. She was haunted by her thoughts and constantly sought answers to questions she had asked many times before. "Why didn't God deliver me from this dysfunctional marriage when I cried for help so many times?" "Why did my Christian friends and family turn their backs on me and become so critical?" She felt abandoned by everyone—her family, her friends, and God. She was angry and bitter, and evil lurked in the shadows, knowing exactly how to fill the gaping hole inside her. There was a cavernous void inside of her, and she began walking down a slippery path that would ultimately lead to destruction.

It seemed so innocent—simple conversations, walking out to the car together, and an occasional phone text—until one day they decided to drive to the mountains. Eden knew in her heart that she was wrong for being alone with another man. His name was Luke. When she was with him, she felt wanted and desirable. His very presence provided warm feelings and luring emotions that she had not felt in years. She also felt a powerful sense of freedom. Luke spent time with her, talking with her and encouraging her in every area of her life. He never said anything discouraging or negative. This was exactly what she had longed for! It was so refreshing, and she was finally beginning to feel attractive again. *This is how a man should treat a woman*, Eden thought to herself. She would share her deepest thoughts with him, and he would listen sympathetically, then offer words of comfort and affirmation. For the first time, she was able to share what she was going through with another person who had empathy and truly seemed to care. "You deserve to be treated like a queen," Luke would say to Eden. His calm demeanor and soothing words would bring tears to her eyes, and she was absolutely captivated.

Although she was enjoying every minute of her new relationship, she realized she was becoming the type of woman she never wanted to be and the woman she never dreamed she would become. Unfortunately, she didn't care anymore. She had lost touch with her real identity and didn't recognize the woman she saw in the mirror. She no longer maintained hope that her life could be better. The promises in the Bible worked for some people but not for her. Deep in her soul, she knew she belonged to God, but she was so angry with Him and His failure to answer her prayers, she decided to jump ship without a life vest. Her desire to have a new life surpassed waiting on God, who clearly was busy helping other people. She was tired of waiting, tired of being trapped in an unhappy, unhealthy marriage. A part of her wanted to completely self-destruct so Heath would agree to a divorce. She was at wit's end, unable to think rationally, ready to risk everything—even her integrity.

Chapter 8

The Unraveling

E<small>DEN'S RELATIONSHIP WITH</small> L<small>UKE</small> continued for several months. It had started as something innocent and brought her much excitement, but it suddenly became very dark and sinful. He claimed to be a Christian, and they had discussed this in depth many times, but as time passed, she discovered that nothing could be further from the truth. He revealed a persona that was defiled, distorted, corrupt, and very immoral. Eden grew increasingly confused and was distraught, realizing that she was extremely frightened of him. He was asking her to do things she had never dreamed of doing. She was appalled, and her mind could barely conceive of the things he was requesting of her. She had trusted him, and she thought he genuinely cared about her! Oddly, even though she knew things were terribly wrong, their relationship seemed to give her a sense of security. She did not want to lose him, and she was afraid to walk away.

One afternoon, Eden and Luke were sitting in a dimly lit room discussing her upcoming figure competition. Luke had been looking at his computer for quite some time when he asked Eden to come and sit beside him; he had something he wanted her to try. As she approached the desk, she noticed four, neatly piled, white lines of a powdery substance. Eden had no idea what it was and began to laugh nervously as she asked, "Okay, what is this?" He calmly answered, "It's cocaine. Just try it." Her heart skipped a beat. She wanted to run out the door and never come back! She had never even taken a sip of alcohol or smoked a cigarette! She certainly had no experience with drugs! "Absolutely not!" Eden answered. Luke snickered in his nonchalant manner and calmly said, "I promise, it is no big deal." He proceeded to explain how to use the drug and assured her it was safe. Maybe she simply wanted to please Luke, but after he demonstrated how to inhale it, Eden did the same. She was instantly addicted!

Eden's life had taken an immediate turn for the worse. She could not get enough of the new drug she had been introduced to. It did not matter how Luke treated her anymore. She knew it was an expensive drug, so if so she continued seeing him, she wouldn't have to pay for the cocaine. She had discovered that when she used the drug, her energy level was high, and perhaps best of all, it suppressed her appetite, and she barely ate anything at all. It was now easy to control her weight! In retrospect, in some distorted way, it seemed that she wanted to secretly destroy herself with this horrible habit. She hated her life, her husband, Luke, and now she hated herself. How she longed to get away from all of it, but she was deep in a pit with no way out. Death would have been welcome, but since that wasn't an option, self-destruction was the next best thing; at least, that's how she felt.

Her drug habit became overwhelming. She would lie awake in bed, strongly desiring the use of the drug. She used it immediately upon awakening, while driving, every time she went into a bathroom, in the tanning bed, before work, during work. She even used it while in the backseat of their van, with her boys sitting in front seat. It did not matter where she was. Before long, she began losing weight and having nosebleeds. Her hands would shake uncontrollably while she held a pen, a glass, or any utensil. Eden could not stop, and she was scared.

On the day of her first National Figure show in Chicago, she was ecstatic. She had worked so hard to get to this competition. This was her first national show since she had won the National Pre-Qualifier Figure Competition. That same weekend, Connor had an appointment to meet with an orthodontist in the same city, so to her dismay, Heath and the boys planned to attend the competition. She really did not want Heath to be there. He made her very nervous, not to mention, she was highly addicted to cocaine, and she was already agitated and anxious.

Prior to the competition, Eden increased the amount of cocaine she was using to lose weight for the competition. The drug also helped her feel better in general, and she wanted to look and feel great for this competition. The drive to Chicago was a very long ten-hour drive. She used the drug in the backseat of their car all day long, so she failed to eat anything. There were three events that weekend—Friday evening, Saturday morning, and the main event was on Saturday evening. She was so stressed with Heath being there. Trying to rid herself of this anxiety, she used too much cocaine before the first show Friday night. Eden was unaware of how much cocaine she had actually used that evening. During the Friday evening show, Eden had completed her first walk across the stage and her first mandatory round of turns. She walked to the side of the stage to stand with the other women until the judging was complete. As she was standing in the women's lineup, two men kindly escorted her off stage. Eden had begun sweating profusely and shaking uncontrollably. The men who escorted her off stage told her she looked very ill, and the judges were afraid she was going to faint, so they kindly dismissed her from the evening show. Eden had no idea her body was exhibiting any of these physical symptoms. She was so humiliated that night, she decided not to return and compete the following day. That was probably an excellent decision, because she had never looked so muscularly soft and weak. She had lost her muscle mass from not eating enough and ingesting too much cocaine. She was so severely disappointed and upset with herself. She had finally made it to a national show, and she blew it, all because she had a stupid, irresponsible, brainless addiction.

When Eden, Heath, and the boys returned home from the competition, she couldn't wait to see Luke. She wanted to tell him that she was having a problem with her cocaine use. When she finally had a chance to talk to him, he just dismissed her concerns and didn't seem to care. Instead, he introduced her to marijuana, hash, and alcohol to help her come down from the high of cocaine. Eden could not believe she had stooped to such levels of sin. She knew better! This was not the life she wanted to live! She had been so rejected in her marriage to Heath, and yet she was choosing to be in a relationship with another man and was living for the high from a destructive drug. Everything about this situation was wrong. Every bad decision took her further and further from the loving mother she once was. Her faith and personal integrity had been annihilated, and she had done it to herself. Her soul was empty, and her heart was cold. She continued to meet Luke several times a week, but after he provided the drugs and she was in a helpless stupor, he would leave her alone in a dark room. The drugs and alcohol made her sick and left her extremely disoriented. She was unstable in every way, making it impossible to drive herself home. She would lie there alone and cry, staring at the ceiling until the side effects would subside and she was able to drive home. Sometimes she would remember Luke's words, "You should be treated like a queen." This definitely didn't feel like royal treatment. "Why would he leave me alone when I'm so sick? Why would he do this to me?" Eden cried.

Meanwhile, Eden was spending less time at home. As soon as her boys came home from school, she would leave to go meet Luke, so she would not see Heath when he came home from work. The boys were still very young and needed Eden at home, but she was more concerned about not being home when Heath arrived. She hated being in the same room with him. He made her so nervous; she avoided him as much as possible. If he did not want a divorce, she was going to be gone as much as she possibly could. Unfortunately, her precious boys suffered as a result of her selfish choices. There were days when the boys begged her not to leave the house, but her desire for cocaine and her hatred for Heath were so overwhelming. Her addictions led her straight out the door and away from her children. Somehow, she was able to extinguish the sounds of her children's voices and their cries. She had no concept of the depth of pain they felt. She was their mother, but her conscience was seared, and her emotions were numb. She was completely empty—dead inside.

"How could a mother not have compassion for her own children?" Eden wondered to herself. She knew she loved them, but why was she unable to pull herself together and take care of them? How did she allow herself to get to this point? That is why she wanted to leave Heath for so long. He was a cold-blooded, heartless person, and now she was acting the same way. There was no one to talk to and nowhere to turn, so she continued with her addiction, numbing the pain with each fix.

Chapter 9

The End of the Beginning

Luke had asked Eden to accompany him on a business trip to the West Coast. It was risky but a risk she was willing to take. She was excited to share this experience with him, because Heath never wanted to do anything with her, nor did he ever plan any vacations with her. Luke purchased their plane tickets, and they attended his business conference and then decided to fly to Las Vegas for a quick fun visit. Luke had never been there and had always wanted to go. Unfortunately, his idea of fun was not the same as hers. Of course, neither Eden nor Luke could travel without their drugs, so they managed to get cocaine and weed through the airport security and onto the plane. Eden was more scared than she had ever been in her life. She had feared being caught with illegal substances, but at the same time, she wasn't sure how she would survive without them.

When they arrived in Vegas, she was ready to see the city, but Luke had other things on his mind. He was living out his own fantasy and decided to rent a presidential suite in one of the largest hotels in the city. It was huge! He was ready to party and wasn't interested in anything else. Inside the suite, Eden sat quietly and began to look carefully at her surroundings. For some reason, she began reminiscing about the vacations she took with her family to

Vegas during her childhood and the innocence of those memorable days. Her family was never able to afford such a large suite like the one Luke had chosen. Now Eden had placed herself in a situation she had never dreamed of, and she didn't want to be there. Suddenly, she was brought back to reality by the sound of Luke's voice. He was starting to demand things from her that truly frightened her. "Why is it that people think anything goes just because they are in Vegas?" Eden wondered. "Sin is sin, no matter where you are!" Luke's requests were immoral, and she was being exposed to a world that was foreign to her. She had no desire to participate in acts that would feed his twisted sinful desires, so fearfully, she told him no.

The darkness in Eden's world had just become totally black. She knew immediately that she needed to get out of this evil pit of hell she had put herself in. Luke never wanted to leave the room; he just wanted to have a huge party, with drugs and other activities that were completely vile.

Finally, Luke left the room to go downstairs. Feeling terrified and unclean, Eden retreated to her safe place, the bathroom, to take a shower. As the warm water cascaded down her face, full of shame and disgrace, she began to cry. She stayed in the shower as long as she could. Then she stepped out, dried herself, and walked over to the large window overlooking the entire strip. "The city that never sleeps, Sin City," Eden said, weeping. She just stood there, feeling totally exposed before God, in all of her sin and shame. Tears flowed endlessly, and she began pouring her heart out to the Savior who had always loved her, whose heart must have been broken as He watched her that afternoon. "Lord, I know I am yours! You know what led me here, but I did not mean to go this far! Please forgive me! Please deliver me from the hell I'm living in! I know I need help, and I know I need to get out to of this situation! Please help me out of this sinful pit, away from Luke and these drugs! I love you, and I am so sorry I have brought shame to you, my boys, and myself!"

"What happens in Vegas stays in Vegas" was not true for Eden! The next morning, she received a phone call from Heath asking where she was and who she was with. As frightened as she was, she knew God had answered her prayer. It was over, and she was going home.

Eden's secret was revealed and out in the open for all to see. She could no longer hide the fact that she was living an immoral life and hooked on drugs. While Eden had been in Las Vegas, Heath had read all of her diaries—from her childhood to the present time. He had looked up all of her phone records and also found the plane tickets Luke had purchased for the trip. She told Luke that Heath knew everything, and there was no longer any way to hide what they were doing, but he was only concerned about himself. He wanted to make sure his name was not going to be dragged through the mud, and he warned her that she must keep her mouth shut about him. He didn't intend to own any blame for her problems, and he wanted her to leave him out of it. Eden quickly gathered her things and took a cab to the airport alone. Luke remained in Vegas to enjoy the rest of his vacation, as though nothing happened. He did, however, provide her with a good amount of cocaine for the trip home. In preparation for her trip, she had tucked a small medicine tube of cocaine in the front pocket of her jeans. While going through airport security, Eden was pulled out of line by an officer who requested that she be given a full body search. She was asked to empty all of her pockets, so she reached in her jeans and put the medicine tube on a chair past the officer and said, "Sorry, I have a headache." The officer just looked at her for a moment with a blank stare, then continued the search. Miraculously, Eden was released and allowed to go to her gate. God's grace and mercy saved her that day. She knew that if she had been caught with the cocaine, she would have gone straight to prison. Unfortunately, Eden was so numb, and her thinking was so clouded, she really didn't care if they did arrest her—but God did!

When she arrived home, there was extreme tension, and things were worse than ever. Eden thought for sure since that if Heath had read all of her diaries, he would now understand how she felt about him. Couldn't he read between the lines enough to see why she had made unwise choices? Wasn't it clear that she had grown weary in their marriage and had just given up?

Apparently not, because while she was out of town, Heath had contacted her parents, her family, her friends, people where she worked, their pastor, and their entire church staff and told them that she was on drugs and having an affair with another man. To make matters worse, Heath also contacted Luke's pastor, the church staff, and his family, telling them the same thing. Unfortunately, in addition to the raw facts, Heath embellished the story by falsifying various events. The true story was bad enough, but he added gory details and made up things that never happened. Every time he told someone else about her corrupt behavior, his story would grow more grandiose. He completely shamed her and embarrassed her, resulting in rumors that were untrue and harmful gossip that added to the fire. Since he did not have all the facts, he decided to create his own version of what really happened. He was working overtime to ensure that people knew what a wonderful man he was and just how difficult it was to be married to a fallen angel.

There was no question that Eden did fall, but she just wished everyone would understand the circumstances preceding the fall. No one knew the thoughtless, verbally malicious man she lived with. She was now the sinful woman, exposed to the community by her husband, who appeared to be the blameless and holy. It was as if Heath swelled with pride as he eagerly waited for each observer to cast stones at her. He was clearly enjoying himself while Eden was pushed further into a black hole of disgrace. His behavior toward her was despicable.

When Luke's party in Las Vegas ended, he returned home to find that his involvement with Eden was not kept quiet, as he had demanded. He was furious about being exposed, but he had no intention of assuming any responsibility. He told his friends, his pastor, and his family that Eden was obsessed with him, that she stalked him, that she was crazy. He denied having a relationship with her and said he had never used drugs and would certainly not have provided them for her.

In an effort to rid herself of guilt, Eden decided to call Luke and ask for his forgiveness so that she could move on with her life. Her involvement with him had been wrong in every way, and she was trying to take responsibility for her own sin. To her dismay, all he requested of her was to never bring up his name again and to keep quiet about everything. She couldn't believe he had no apology for her and didn't seem to think he had done anything that required forgiveness from her. Why was it acceptable that her reputation was destroyed, but his good name needed to be protected? From his perspective, he had a business, reputable character, a wife, and family he was trying to protect; therefore, she should never reveal anything that happened between them! Eden had disclosed everything about herself; she had owned her bad choices, and she felt totally exposed to the whole world. But she chose not to deny the ugly truth, realizing that the only way she could be restored was to learn from her mistakes and try to start over again. The only things she denied were the false, imaginary details that Heath concocted in his mind.

Chapter 10

The Long Journey Back

Luke was no longer in Eden's life, for which she was so thankful. However, when she ended the relationship with him, she lost her drug supplier. He had given her drugs from the time that she met him, and now she was going through major withdrawal. She had depended on cocaine to help her get through her long days and even longer nights. It helped her deal with pain and personal struggles. It made her feel good, thin, beautiful, and confident. Now, there was no access, and her craving for the drug was stronger than ever. The turmoil and stress at home was almost more than she could bear, and she had nothing to help her cope. Withdrawing from the drug had made her weak, sick, and severely depressed. Heath had talked to her family, so they knew how sick she was and decided to come and help.

Eden would never forget the looks of disappointment and utter shock on their faces when they saw her. The memory of that visit was absolutely heartbreaking. They all sat down with her at the kitchen table, and she began to share everything she had been through. She tried to explain how terrible her marriage to Heath had been, and she told them how he continued to hurt her and neglect her. It was evident that no matter what she said, they still didn't believe her. No one ever believed anything negative about Heath! Besides, her transgression far surpassed any other finger pointing at this stage of the game. She had waited far too long to tell her family the truth about Heath; instead, she just medicated her pain and withdrew from everyone—even her own children. She had jumped off the cliff, almost fatally wounded herself, but had been rescued and was trying to recover from the treacherous fall. The only things that mattered now were her family and, most of all, her relationship with God.

As they were talking at the table that evening, Eden noticed a small white particle in the center of the table. Instinctively, she quickly reached out and pressed on it gently to bring it to her nose. She suddenly stopped herself as she realized what she had done. It was a white speck of drywall, and everyone at the table knew what had happened. With watery eyes, they gazed at her sadly as Eden sat quietly, completely humiliated, and in total disbelief. Her habit was so out of control; anything resembling cocaine went in her nose. Eden began to cry and humbly begged for their help.

Eden had to seek help for her addiction. A counselor had referred her to a rehabilitation center several states away, but she didn't have the money to go. The treatment would cost thousands of dollars, so she decided to do it on her own, asking God to help her every step of the way. She thought it would be helpful if she stayed with her parents for a few weeks, and they agreed. She asked for time off from work, said good-bye to her boys, and went home with her parents.

While she was gone, Heath continued to call her friends at work, trying to find out anything they might know that he didn't. He read through her diaries again, rummaged through her clothes, searched through personal items, and even looked for bills, receipts, and more. He even threatened to burn some of her clothes that he didn't want her wearing for anyone else but him. He continued to talk to the church staff members and spread rumors throughout the church about her drug use and her relationship with Luke. Occasionally, Heath would call her on the phone and accuse her of things she had never done. He would blame her for things she hadn't done and question her about incidents in her diaries that had been recorded ten years before she had met him. He would remind her that she had never been a submissive wife or a good mother to his children and that her actions proved it. She was trying desperately to heal from her addiction, and she longed to put the past behind her. When she listened to his accusing voice on the phone, it was doubly hard to pick herself up and keep moving forward. Sometimes she would remind Heath of the events that had preceded the bad choices she made. If she was such an embarrassment to him, why wouldn't he give her a divorce? Then he could move on with his perfect, Godly life, and she could take her broken, unworthy self somewhere else. It made no sense. He wanted everyone to know how "bad," she was, but he was playing "hero" by allowing her to live under his roof. Her parents were beginning to get a glimpse of the true character of the man she married.

Five weeks later, Eden decided it was time to go home. She had made it without cocaine for thirty-five days and was beginning to feel healthy again. She knew she didn't have easy access to the drug, but a lot still depended on her ability to say no. The cravings were still there, but with each passing day, she grew stronger and had more confidence in herself. It was time for her to get back to her boys, and unfortunately, that meant she had to go back to Heath. She had planned on having a friend take her home from the airport, but due to her work schedule, it didn't work out. Instead, her friend's boyfriend, Mark, was coming to get her.

Eden had a nice flight home, but she was really nervous about going home. She was unsure of how Heath was going to treat her and what situations she might encounter. She feared what he might have told the boys about her and how they would react when they saw her.

Eden dreaded the walk down the corridor to the baggage

claim. Every step was taking her closer to Heath and a very volatile situation at home. When she arrived in the baggage claim area, she saw Mark sitting in a chair nearby, waiting for her to arrive so he could drive her home. They greeted each other and waited for Eden's luggage. Mark lifted her suitcase from the conveyor belt, and as they turned to leave from the baggage claim area, she saw Heath. There he was, secretly taking pictures through the glass doors of the airport, trying to catch her with someone she was not supposed to be with. When Heath realized she had seen him, he charged through the sliding glass doors and ordered her to get in his car. Mark stood there in amazement. She told Heath that she had a ride and that he was far too angry for her to get in the car with him. She wasn't riding home with him. Heath was very angry and approached her, standing very close to her face. Mark stepped up to get between them and informed Heath that she was riding home with him. Heath created such a scene that it captured the attention of the police. Heath decided to leave before being escorted out of the airport. Eden was so grateful that Mark had been there to help her and take her home. Although she was completely humiliated, she was very pleased she had stood up for herself. Heath's hateful, erratic behavior was finally revealed to others!

The ride home with Mark was very quiet. Eden was embarrassed about the encounter with Heath, and she was scared to go home and face her family. Questions flooded Eden's head. *What do my boys think of me for being gone for so long? What has Heath been telling them about me?* She found herself craving the energy provided by the little white powder she no longer had. How was she going to handle the stressful situations that were imminent? The desire to use the drug was so powerful, but she reminded herself that the addiction had robbed her of her health, time with her boys, and her relationship with God. She was determined to stay clean. She was strong and courageous; God would help her! She remembered something she had heard when she was a teenager, and it was so true. She had believed it and repeated it, but now she was living it, and as a result, she lost two years of precious time.

> "Sin—it will take you farther than you want to go,
> Make you stay longer than you want to stay,
> And cost you more than you want to pay."

Chapter 11

Mirror Image

Eden stood motionless as she gazed at her herself in the mirror. She was extremely thin and looked so frail and vulnerable. Above the mirror hung four light fixtures that brilliantly illuminated her protruding skeletal frame and pale, sallow skin. Her bloodshot eyes were framed with baggy skin from sleepless nights and days of weeping. She was particularly disturbed by the lack of expression on her face. She appeared empty and emotionless. "Who is this?" Eden cried aloud as she stared with disgust at herself in the mirror. "What have I done?" she screamed. Feeling repulsed and sickened by her own image, she stepped away from the mirror. *Will I ever be the same again? It's impossible,* she thought. Eden had lost everything—her boys, her home, her integrity, her beauty, her finances, her friends, and most of all her relationship with God.

She did not write in her diary for two years. There was nothing that she wanted to put on paper. During this period when she descended into the devil's darkness, she had no desire to describe her daily activities in a diary. She had been consumed by apathy, allowing drugs and other destructive habits to wreck her life. She was aware of the precious years that were wasted due to her sinful choices, and she had no written recollection, just dark memories.

Even though she had fallen into the deepest pit of darkness, she knew God would bring everything into the light, because she belonged to Him. She thought about the scripture in Ecclesiastes 12:14, "For God will bring every deed into judgment, including every hidden thing, whether it is good or evil." This verse confirmed her relationship with God, but the tremendous extent of shame, guilt, and disgrace that possessed her was overwhelming. Her family and friends didn't understand. It seemed easy enough. She should just pray and ask for forgiveness, then move forward and never look back. It wasn't that simple! When she tried to pray, she felt too ashamed to ask for anything. She was afraid that she had marred her testimony in a manner that was unrecoverable. Once again, she truly longed to die. It seemed to be the only solution—a quick ending to the crippling pain she felt.

One of the most difficult realities for Eden involved the fact that she had hurt many innocent people. Her sweet little boys did not deserve the pain they must have endured. There were so many times when she wasn't home to care for them. There must have been many times when they needed the nurturing love of a mother, and she was absent. These truths were gut wrenching, and she grieved endlessly.

She was also dealing with extreme anger toward the people who had deliberately hurt her. Heath and Luke were at the forefront of her anger, but there were others. She was dumbfounded by the reactions of those who were supposedly her Christian friends and had served with her in ministry. They all disappeared—not a phone call, not a text, not a visit, not a word from any of them. It was as if she was dead to them, too sinful for them to associate with. The saddest thing was that no one took the time to reach out to her in an attempt to understand the reason behind her sudden deviant behavior. No one extended a hand or offered to help her find her way back. Instead, they assumed the worst, spread rumors, pointed fingers, and whispered behind her back.

November 7, 2007
Dear Diary,

Wow—two years since I've written. A lot has happened. I got involved with a man from the gym, and he introduced me to cocaine, weed, and alcohol, not to mention many things I don't even want to write out. I got caught; all was exposed, and this man walked free! And he called me crazy! I was stalked and haunted by Heath every day for months. It was horrible. Then finally I got a divorce in July.

Eden and Heath's situation had elevated so severely that she had to leave their home, and unfortunately, she had to leave without her boys. She did not want to leave her precious boys behind, but she had no way of financially supporting herself, much less three growing boys. Heath had refused to leave, and it was unsafe for her to stay with him, so she left because she felt there was no other option. She moved in with a friend who had a temporary room. Eden decided to meet with a lawyer about a week later, and Heath finally agreed to a divorce. She refused any financial support from Heath, because she didn't want him to have any type of control over her anymore. However, she didn't have a permanent place to live and no income to pay her bills. She was homeless, broken, and alone, but from deep inside her, there was a new determination to make it on her own. She didn't know how it would happen, but she would get back on her feet, and she would be fine. She was determined to do whatever it took, and oddly enough, for the first time in sixteen years, she felt that she could breathe freely!

Eden stayed with her friend for three months—a gesture of kindness from one person that she never forgot. She worked whenever and wherever she could, teaching aerobic classes, cleaning houses, and serving as a waitress. For seven long years after the divorce, she struggled, trying to make ends meet and merely survive. There were many days that she could not afford to buy anything to eat. She recalled one specific incident when she opened her pantry and found a couple of cans of soup, but she didn't have a can opener or useful utensil, nor did she have the money to go buy one. Frequently, she deprived herself of food so she could buy gas or pay her bills. Eden would often think of the days when she and Heath were in school and she had stood in line for hours with her boys, just to get free food. Her situation was different now, and she didn't know where to go or who to turn to for help. Friends were few, and she didn't trust many people, certainly not enough to ask for help.

She moved nine times in seven years, due to various reasons and circumstances. She was barely existing, physically and emotionally. Her greatest sorrow was not being at home with her boys. She would not have hurt more if someone had actually thrust a dagger through her heart. Not only did she struggle with being separated from them, she was well aware that they were struggling also. Their mom was gone from their home; their dad had nothing good to say about their mom. What a terrible situation for three boys who had no voice in matters related to their home life.

Time was slowly mending the relationships with Eden and her boys, but she had broken their hearts, and she knew there would be permanent repercussions. She accepted the fact that she had brought pain and suffering to them; she owned it. However, she also knew that their dad had played a huge role in the shattering of their family, and she longed for them to know the whole truth. She did not just walk out on them because she was selfishly pursuing some exciting venture on her own. It wasn't that simple. As a matter of fact, it was quite complicated, but she could never find a way to fully explain it. Most of the time, she just kept silent. She was making every effort to spend time with James, Connor, and Ronan attempting to provide the love and nurturing they had missed from her. Through it all, she was still dealing with severe depression and guilt. At this point in her life, she was totally living for her children. Without them, her circumstances would have plunged her completely in the depths of despair. She was angry with her circumstances that had led her down the path of destruction, even though she knew the bad choices were hers. She constantly asked God, "How can I help my children mend if I am broken?"

Several years had passed since the divorce, and she was free from the drug that had once possessed her mind and body. But she was far from whole. By now, she expected that she would have been restored and back on her feet. She thought she would have experienced total inner healing. Instead, she continued to view herself as a scorned woman that no one wanted to be around. She still hadn't heard from anyone at church, and none of her former "friends" seemed to care that she was desperately fighting for her existence. She longed for someone to pray for her and with her, but it never happened. Heath had done a fabulous job turning people against her. Meanwhile, he kept attending church and living the good life. He was well respected, and everyone felt sorry for him. Eden's bitterness grew deeper every time she thought about what he did to their family and to her.

From her childhood, Eden knew that all of life's most complex problems could be solved inside the realms of a relationship with God. She truly believed it, but she was so wounded by Christians that she couldn't bring herself to step inside a church. She tried to pray, but there always seemed to be a very thick wall between her and God. She hoped that one day she would desire to grow as a Christian again, but she wanted her spiritual growth to be different and unconventional—growth that had a new foundation, built by God alone and not people. Eden wanted to grow at her own pace, not at the pace set by others and based on the opinions of those around her. She wanted her faith to be solid, true, and unwavering. She also knew that if she was going to find true forgiveness and peace in her life again, she needed to pick up her Bible and read it! Finally, Eden was able to open her Bible, and she began to read.

Immediately, she felt burning tears flood her eyes as she turned the pages to Psalms 142:2–7 and read, "I pour out before Him my complaint; before Him I tell my trouble. When my spirit grows faint within me, it is You who watch over my way. In the path where I walk people have hidden a snare for me. Look and see, there is no one at my right hand, no one is concerned for me. I have no refuge; no one cares for my life. I cry to you, Lord; I say, 'You are my refuge, my portion in the land of the living.' Listen to my cry, for I am in desperate need; rescue me from those who pursue me, for they are too strong for me. Set me free from my prison, that I may praise your name. Then the righteous will gather about me because of your goodness to me."

Eden was exhausted from years of struggling, financially and spiritually. She wanted off the emotional roller coaster that was making her physically sick. She had spent the last two of years in and out of doctors' offices with various illnesses as a result of her stress. She had attempted to relinquish her anger, bitterness, and guilt to the Lord. She began to ask Him to forgive her for all of her sins and give her relief from her guilt. She also asked for help releasing the anger she felt toward Heath, friends, and family who had disappointed her, and especially the anger she felt for herself.

Even though Eden had asked for forgiveness, she realized she had created a self-induced or self-inflicted negative mind-set where she consistently told herself, "I will never be used by God again," and, "I will never be good enough. God has removed His blessing from me, and there is no longer a purpose for me." Not only did she dwell on these thoughts and constantly berate herself, she had also been told by other people that her life was "ruined" and that God would not use her again. She was told that her sinful choices had resulted in the loss of God's purpose and direction for her and that God would never use her the way He had "originally planned." So what was God going to do with her, if anything? Then she remembered something that made a profound difference. Romans

3:23 says, "For all have sinned and come short of the Glory of God." So Eden began to wonder. If all have sinned, what sin is so bad in the eyes of God that would cause Him to change His plan for that person's life? She thought of Jesus's death on the cross and wondered what He must have endured when He bore all the sins of the world. He knew the type of sins we would commit; He knew what the consequences would be; He knew what those sins felt like. He bore them all! She began to grasp the fact that God felt her struggle with cocaine; He felt her pain when she was spoken to in an ugly way; He felt her guilt when she made corrupt choices. He knew exactly how she felt!

Eden claimed the prayer of David, Psalm 51:1–4, "Have mercy upon me, O God, according to Your loving kindness; According to the multitude of Your tender mercies, Blot out my transgressions. Wash me thoroughly from my iniquity, and cleanse me from my sin. For I acknowledge my transgressions, and my sin is always before me. Against You, You only, have I sinned. And done this evil in Your sight—That You may be found just when You speak, and blameless when You judge."

Eden was drained and exhausted from feeling sorry for herself. Self-pity had consumed her mind, body, and soul. She was through beating herself up. She refused to cry or be ashamed about anything God could use for His glory. Eden could not change the past, but neither was she going to allow her past to destroy her. She had asked for His forgiveness and to be cleansed and made whole again. She wanted to feel accepted, worthy, beautiful, respected, deserving, and valuable again. Only the Lord could do this for her.

Psalm 51:7–13 says, "Purge me with hyssop, and I will be clean; Wash me, and I shall be whiter than snow. Make me hear joy and gladness, that the bones You have broken may rejoice. Hide Your face from my sins, and blot our all my iniquities. Create in me a clean heart, O God, and renew a steadfast spirit within me. Do not cast me away from Your presence, And do not take Your Holy Spirit from me. Restore to me the joy of Your salvation, And uphold me by Your salvation, And uphold me by Your generous Spirit. Then I will teach transgressors Your ways, And sinners shall be converted to You."

Eden realized that she was a steward of her body, and she needed to take care of herself for Him. He was living inside her, and her body belonged to Him. She had always lacked self-esteem, and feelings of self-worth were nonexistent. When she appeared confident and sure of herself, it was all false. She knew that true confidence is found in Christ, and she didn't allow Him to provide this for her. Eden didn't want to be like the plastic flowers—fake throughout every season, never showing true colors and having no fragrance. She wanted to be like the rose—real and beautiful, full of fragrance. God created the rose with its many thorns, and the thorns don't affect the beauty of the rose or its sweet aroma. Man created the plastic flower, but its beauty was not genuine, and it never provided any pleasant aromas. She wanted to be real, not fake!

God did have a purpose for her life, regardless of her past sins and poor decisions! She knew He had given her another opportunity to serve Him. She never wanted to underestimate the potential He had given her. She knew He could use her to be a blessing to others; she just wasn't sure how He would do it. The years she thought she had lost, God promised to return if she followed Him. Joel 2:25 says, "I will repay you for the years the locusts have eaten."

Chapter 12

The New Beginning

God had truly sustained Eden through many years of adversity and suffering. One at a time, she made good choices and worked diligently on loving herself again. She was relentless in her pursuit of stability and prosperity. Best of all, she met a wonderful man who loved her unconditionally and accepted her just as she was. He knew all of her past struggles, but they were of no significance to him. He thought she was beautiful and worthy of honor and treated her accordingly. They were now happily married, and her relationships with James, Connor, and Ronan had been restored.

Eden had two part-time jobs that enabled her to contribute financially to their new family but soon found this situation to be physically demanding. Unfortunately, she sustained a back injury—a large herniated disc that resulted in surgery to remove it. She resigned from one job due to job restrictions but remained in the fitness field that she enjoyed very much. While she was out recovering from the surgery, she had plenty of time to think and plan. She found herself praying for a new ministry opportunity. She was still seeking to find God's plan for her life, not wanting her past experiences to have been in vain. She knew God could use her testimony to help others; she just didn't know how it would happen.

Finally, after all these years, she was able to fully understand that God forgave her the first time she asked. Her inner guilt and inability to forgive herself resulted in repeated prayers, asking for forgiveness of the sins in her past. She never "felt" forgiven, so she kept on asking. In 1 John 1:9, it says, "If we confess our sins, He is faithful and just to forgive our sins and cleanse us from all unrighteousness." She did not need to ask over and over again! It was that simple! He told her to ask for forgiveness; she asked Him; He forgave. End of story! In doing so, He took away the guilt, shame, anger, bitterness, resentment, and unresolved emotion. She simply had to relinquish them and place them forever in His hands. Eden was free! God's forgiveness had made her pure and white as snow! She was no longer a slave to sin, imprisoned by unhappiness, resentment, and anger. The ugliness had been washed away, and God had made her whole again. God had taken a fading plastic flower and created a beautiful rose, full of fragrance, and yes, thorns! When Eden would reflect on all the events in her life, she was always reminded of the cross Jesus bore for her! What horrendous physical and emotional pain He endured as He carried the burden of sin for the entire world—the sins of each and every person! He understood what sin did to people; He knew how big the scars could be; He knew the depth of sorrow that we would experience when we sin. His death on the cross bought forgiveness and life for people like her! Psalms 103:12 says, "As far as the east is from the west, so far has he removed our transgressions from us." She was filled with unspeakable joy when she read this.

Eden could finally see that God could take something totally ugly and make it beautiful. She knew that there would be other times when she would sin, but she rested in the knowledge that when she repented, God would forgive and restore. No more regrets, no more remorse, no more tears. Eden's prison walls had finally been torn down, and her diva days were over. Her need to look a certain way or behave according to the standards of others had diminished. She was no longer bound by chains of perfection and unrealistic personal expectations. Heath's abusive words that fueled her feelings of inadequacy were now just a bad memory, and she knew they were lies.

James had met the girl of his dreams, and they were getting married. At the rehearsal dinner, Eden looked around the room, beautifully lit with candles and rope lighting. The ceiling was a wavy sea of gorgeous, silk white fabric. Each table was heavily adorned with elegant place settings and beautiful decorations. Family and friends were all around, enjoying the enchanting atmosphere and engaging in intimate conversations. As she took it all in, she was aware of the myriad of powerful emotions that flooded her thoughts. She smiled! God had restored the emotions and feelings she had lost for years. In fact, they were so strong, it was almost more than she could fathom. While listening to the diverse conversations at the table, her eyes were intently fixed on the stage where this memorable event would take place. Her mind drifted, and she began reminiscing about James's childhood. She was abruptly brought back to reality by the sweet sound of her son's voice. "Mom, Mom! Are you ready? It's time to go!" Her firstborn baby was getting married tomorrow, and he had asked her to sing at his wedding. It would be the first time she had sung in ten years! She was extremely anxious but also very excited and blessed to be a part in this extraordinary event. Eden needed to practice her song. She wanted everything to be perfect!

Wedding day arrived, and Eden stood in front of the mirror, staring at her reflection. She saw a tall, slender, young woman that she hardly recognized. Her newly styled hair fell loosely on tanned shoulders. Her eyes were luminous, and her face was radiant. She was no longer bound by the chains of her past or driven by the expectations of others. She was new again! She was beautiful again, because Christ made her that way! Psalms 34:5 says, "Those who look to Him are radiant; their faces are never covered with shame."

She was new again! Eden took one last glance at herself in the mirror before leaving the room—once considered her safe place. She laughed and thought, *So who was the Prison Diva in my dream?* The title was a perfect description of her—a woman who had once desired perfection on stage as a Christian "diva" yet truly lived in a prison off stage. The Prison Diva, she was the one who ... is no more!

Epilogue

God had given Eden a dream, revealing to her the title for this book. In her dream, the hairdresser actually answered her question, "Just who is the Prison Diva?" Her dream ended with a word that unmistakably described the most difficult tribulations Eden could have ever imagined. Upon awakening from her dream, she was hesitant to type the descriptive word that was spoken to her, so she left it blank. God soon revealed to her that she needed to share her testimony through the writing of this book. This missing word at the end of the sentence remains untold for a reason. Eden was no longer defined or held captive by that word, and she did not want to open that chapter of her life again or allow it to be used against her for any reason.

We have all been hurt at some time in our lives, but when the pain and guilt start to define who we are, we put ourselves behind bars in a self-made prison. We feel trapped by our own circumstances and doomed to malicious consequences imposed by those who hurt us. We are unable to find a healthy escape, and we often reject support from sources that would help us break free. Most of all, we fail to see and feel God's forgiveness. This prohibits us from forgiving ourselves and others, leading to a downward spiral that takes us further away from the person we want to be. We must remember that as children of God, every hardship we endure, every damaging relationship we cultivate, and every harmful word that is said, passes through the hands of the Almighty God, our Father, who loves us in spite of our failures. He uses each of His children for His glory when repentance takes place and the child returns to Him. That beautiful restoration generates a unique testimony of grace and hope. All who return to Him can be used to bring honor to His name and impact the lives of others. The choice is ours!